SAVVY
NETWORKING

Also by Andrea R. Nierenberg

Nonstop Networking: How to Improve Your Life, Luck and Career
(Capital, 2001)
*Million Dollar Networking: The Sure Way to Find, Grow and Keep Your
Business* (Capital, 2005)

OTHER TITLES IN THE
CAPITAL IDEAS FOR BUSINESS AND PERSONAL DEVELOPMENT SERIES:

THE 10 LENSES: Your Guide to Living & Working in a Multicultural World
by Mark A. Williams

BE HEARD THE FIRST TIME: The Woman's Guide to Powerful Speaking
by Susan Miller

FIT IN! The Unofficial Guide to Corporate Culture by Mark A. Williams

MANAGER MECHANICS: People Skills for First-Time Managers by Eric P. Bloom

MENTAL AGILITY: The Path to Persuasion by Robert L. Jolles

THE NEW TALK POWER: The Mind-Body Way to Speak like a Pro
by Natalie H. Rogers

NOW WHAT DO I DO? The Woman's Guide to a New Career by Jan Cannon

THE POWER OF HANDSHAKING: For Peak Performance Worldwide
by Robert E. Brown and Dorothea Johnson

SAVVY INTERVIEWING: How to Ace the Interview & Get the Job
by John Van Devender and Gloria Van Devender-Graves

*THE SAVVY PART-TIME PROFESSIONAL: How to Land, Create, or Negotiate the
Part-Time Job of Your Dreams* by Lynn Berger

SOLD! Direct Marketing for the Real Estate Pro by Louis K. Geller

YOUR IDENTITY ZONES: Who Am I? Who Are You? How Do We Get Along?
by Mark A. Williams

Save 25% when you order any of these and other fine Capital titles from our
Web site: www.capital-books.com.

SAVVY
NETWORKING

118
Fast & Effective
Tips for
Business Success

Andrea R. Nierenberg

Capital Ideas for Business & Personal Development

CAPITAL
BOOKS, INC.
Sterling, Virginia

Capital Books, Inc.
P.O. Box 605
Herndon, Virginia 20172-0605

ISBN 13: 978-1-933102-44-3 (alk. paper)

Library of Congress Cataloging-in-Publication Data
Nierenberg, Andrea R.
  Savvy networking : fast & effective tips for business success / Andrea R. Nierenberg. — 1st ed.
      p. cm. — (Capital ideas for business & personal development series)
    Includes index.
    ISBN 978-1-933102-44-3 (alk. paper)
    1. Business networks. I. Title. II. Series.

    HD69.58N544 2007
    650.1'3—dc22

                                    2007013203

Printed in the United States of America on acid-free paper that meets the American National Standards Institute 239-48 Standard.

First Edition

10 9 8 7 6 5 4 3 2 1

This book is dedicated to the two people
who have had the most influence on my life
and continue to as they now reside in Heaven
—my dear and wonderful parents
Molly and Paul.
I love you both—
thank you for all the great lessons
of life you taught me.
I think of you both every day.

Contents

Acknowledgments

This is always the hardest page in the book for me to write. There are so many people I am fortunate to have in my life, and I want to thank each of them for their support, encouragement and help in writing *Savvy Networking*.

First and foremost to my wonderful publisher, Kathleen Hughes, who has published all three of my books at Capital and really did everything to make this book come together. Kathleen, you are truly amazing! Thank you! Also to the wonderful staff at Capital and to Jane Graf for her help in getting the book out to the channels of distribution.

To all the great people who gave me wonderful stories that flow throughout the book and added such impact, and to all of you who have touched my life in so many ways. I wish I could write every name down—however, that would be longer than the whole book!

The people who stand out are: JoAnn Accarino, Arlene Adler, Vicky Amon, Elisa Balabram, Rick Botthof, Joni Bradley, Judith Cavaliere, Eric Chandler, Tom Ciesielka, Denise Clancy, Geoffrey Close, Todd Cherches, John Corwin, Diane Danielson, Nathan DeVore, Bruce Dorskind, Bob Drucker, Deborah Fain, Michael Faulkner, Eileen Finn, John Folchetti, Margie Kraker Funch, Carl Gambino, Lauren Garvey, Steve Georgeou, Paul Hansen, Joel Kessler, Don Klein, Dan Koifman, Joyce Ellen Kuras, Robert Lamb, Jon Lambert, Roger Lewis, Laney Liner, Mary Mayotte, John Mazzaraco, Marshall Mermell, Bruce Meyer, Nicole Meyer, Allan Miller, Rick Miners, Trudy and Bill Mitchell, Joyce Newman,

John Ng, Daniel O'Conner, Phil Parrotta, Elaine Pofeldt, Jeff Reinhardt, Ryan Richt, Nick Risom, Gil Robinov, Bernie Rubin, Jeri Sedlar, Bill Snyder, Sheryl Spanier, Scott Swedenburg, Jason Peter Torres, Prakash Venkataraman, Stephen Woeber, and Annmarie Woods.

A special thank you to my dear friend, Lois Geller, who has always been an inspiration to my writing through her terrific books.

I also have a special thanks for my friend Paul Schaye who is a true inspiration to everyone whose life he touches.

Four very dear friends encouraged me who are looking down from heaven where they were taken much too soon: Dick Borzumato, Bruce Eswein, Betty Most, and Robert Schachat.

Finally to my dear brother Richard and sister Meredith—thanks to you both for your continual support. Now that Mom and Dad are up in Heaven, we have become even closer.

Preface
How to Use this Book

One of my missions in life is to show people that networking is a positive word. My first two books—*Nonstop Networking* and *Million Dollar Networking*—convinced a lot of successful people that networking is a vital tool for building long term relationships.

Now I hope that *Savvy Networking* will give my committed readers a refresher course and encourage them to implement some of the ways for connecting and reconnecting with people in their life now, and those they may have not nurtured well enough. I love this quote by Somerset Maugham: "Only a mediocre person is always at his best."

For my new readers, there is a wealth of knowledge about the art of networking and relationship marketing—in quick "sound bites" for easy reading and easy practicing.

Savvy Networking is not meant to be a ponderous reference guide. Instead, it is a selection of my top tips organized into chapters that represent logical steps for building a powerful network —starting with you. You don't need to start at the beginning. For instance, maybe you already feel confident about your self-marketing tools and want to use the book to meet some new friends, start with chapter 4. Throughout the book I've added stories from top networkers who've read my previous books and wanted to share their experiences. Here is one of my favorites from my dear friend, Lois Geller, president of Mason & Geller Direct:

About 20 years ago I was taking the Dale Carnegie Course
in New York City, because I was painfully shy, and my knees

would shake when I had to make a presentation. My boss at Better Homes and Gardens signed me up, and I loved the course. And, because I'd made so much progress, they invited me to become an instructor.

I was again the most nervous in the class. I couldn't remember my name, no less the sessions and the titles and the audience. My brain would freeze up, and I'd muddle through the class and be happy when it was over. The best speaker, presenter in the class was a natural and she worked at helping me through this challenge. She spoke so beautifully, remembered everything, and always had time to give me some advice.

Her name? Andrea Nierenberg. She's still my best friend today, and still helps me out with all kinds of ideas and advice. It is the best of networking, when you make a friend for life.

—Lois K. Geller, Mason & Geller Direct

I do recommend taking on one challenge at a time. Too often when we try to do too much, nothing happens. We get frustrated and don't accomplish anything. My motto is: "To do two things at once is to do neither well." My friend Daniel always says: "You don't 'get it' until you 'do it.'" He started his networking adventure by "being present" at everything—from industry events to in-house management meetings. As he met people and reached out to them, he realized, "I have to be the one to take the initiative and start the process."

As I say in all of my workshops and speeches: It takes time to develop and see the results of your efforts. Yet in this book, knowing your time constraints, we have digested and synthesized all of the tips and techniques into bite-size action plans.

Pick any page, read a tip, and put it into action. In fact, for someone who is traveling, you can read something in Los Angeles and put it into action by the time you reach Chicago.

While everyone needs to network at their own pace, I have three main recommendations:

1. Create your own order. When someone asks me where to start, I say, "Anywhere." The point is to just "do it" the way

you work best—which is the only way it will work. For instance, instead of trying to tackle the entire book at once, pick any tip or topic and concentrate on that one. One of my clients told me that she randomly opens a page in one of my last two books and just reads that page. "Somehow I find the technique to implement something I am working on," she says. If this is the kind of inspiration you need, pick one chapter and dive in. There is no order, you create your own order as you go along.

2. Know where you came from and where you are going. Set goals for how you want to work with new friends and business acquaintances to build a business or personal network.

3. Get into the habit of networking. Once you've learned the basics, you'll no longer feel shy or awkward. You'll enjoy meeting people and giving to them as much as they may give to you. Your network is your community, and you are an integral part of it.

Every tip in this book is timeless. Human nature has always been the same, and networking involves people skills that have been proven over the centuries. In *Savvy Networking,* I give you the insights into people, then it's up to you to implement these skills to meet new people. E-mail, cell phones, instant messaging, and other new technologies have sped up the efficiency and frequency of our communications. Yet it's still the old interpersonal, in-person techniques that are most effective; and using these skills constantly and consistently is what makes them work.

On a personal note, why did I choose 118 for the number of tips I'm passing along to you in this book? First of all, I wanted to give you just one or two tips in bite-size pieces you can think about and use, a week at a time. On another level, the number is symbolic for me. In the Jewish religion, 18 stands for life and luck—which I certainly wish you from the relationships you'll build with this book. And, I confess, I'm a little superstitious. In numerology, 1 is always a new beginning, focused concentration, goal striving and action—all the areas that are addressed in this book.

Following that, 8 is achievement, abundance, self-discipline, power, and strength. I figured putting this all together made for a great and exciting combination. High points of my own career have been the article in which I was featured in *The Wall St Journal* on April 18 and in the *New York Times* on May 18. Then as I was contemplating this title on a recent trip, I got off the hotel elevator and discovered that my hotel room was 118! That cinched it for me.

Introduction
Networking Is About Giving First

> Beginning today, treat everyone you meet as if they were going to be dead by midnight. Extend to them all the care, kindness and understanding you can muster, with no thought of any reward. Your life will never be the same again.
>
> —Og Mandino

Think of the amazing power you'll gain from following the advice in this quote: You will always feel better about yourself and you might make someone else feel better also. This can do a lot not only for your business but also for your life. It goes with my other favorite saying: Give without remembering and receive without forgetting.

Start right now by thinking of someone to whom you can reach out and help—with a business lead or reference, or a simple kindness or a compliment. Make sure that whenever you receive anything—no matter how small—you immediately reach back and thank the other person by note, call, e-mail, or gift and maybe a combination of them.

I was recently talking with Joel, a dear friend and former boss, who said: "We know when we are coming into the world; we just don't know when we are leaving. That is why I say to live each day and be kind to each person you meet."

Or, as my wonderful dad said every day while he was on earth and still says to me as he looks down from Heaven, "Honey, give everyone you meet a smile and a handshake." In going through his things after his death, my mother and I came across this list of life lessons that he had written down.

- ⊙ Listen with your inner ear.
- ⊙ Hear what is said with the heart, rather than what is said with words.
- ⊙ Listen to the concerns of others.
- ⊙ Know when it is important to just listen.
- ⊙ Communication is hard work.
- ⊙ Hone your skills.
- ⊙ State your thoughts clearly and briefly.
- ⊙ Remember to smile, not scowl.
- ⊙ Above all, be reasonable and understanding.
- ⊙ Be interesting and interested.
- ⊙ Be friendly and enthusiastic.
- ⊙ Have a sense of humor.
- ⊙ Be human.
- ⊙ Laugh and grin.

If you had known him, you would recognize that he lived these lines every day.

"Kindness is a language which the deaf can hear and the blind can read," said Mark Twain. Mother Theresa expressed it this way: "Kind words can be short and easy to speak—and their echoes are truly endless."

How can kindness translate into business? Remember, whether you are aware of it or not, no matter what your responsibilities are in the organization, you are in one way or another in "sales," and you'll be more successful when you try to communicate your ideas if you treat everyone like your best customer. Here are some ways to do that: Learn where you fit in your organization. Even it you do not serve customers directly, become familiar with skills that create friendly, professional, dependable customer service.

1. Answer the telephone promptly and respond quickly to requests, demonstrating to others that you are dependable—just as you do with your e-mail.
2. Create a definition of quality service that has meaning for you.

3. Learn to adapt basic customer service skills to the way you treat the "customer" who works alongside you—your co-worker.
4. Go the extra mile to help.
5. Know thy customer!
6. Cater to customer needs.
7. Know that courtesy is always—and will always be—in style.
8. Always be prepared.

This is one of my favorite "kindness pays off" networking stories.

A human resources client of mine asked me to meet with a friend of hers (let's call her Jane) who, as the head of HR for an organization that was in play, was at risk of losing her own job. When Jane and I met, she had a terrible cold. Despite a fever and the threat to her own professional position, Jane focused on what could be done for her company's executives and staff as a result of the buyout. We spent over an hour laying out all the options and I encouraged her to think about her own career and personal needs during the transition as well.

I was so touched by Jane's generosity and professional commitment that I continued to think about her for the rest of the day. On my way home, I stopped in the drug store to pick up a few items and saw some very beautifully wrapped cough drops. The next day, I sent them over with a note: "Chicken soup doesn't mail well . . . but I thought this might help."

Jane immediately responded, told me she had spoken to many consultants who were trying to "sell" her outplacement services, and chose to work with me because I was mainly concerned with her! Over the years, Jane and I have worked together on many projects. She has been a loyal client and a very dear friend.
—Sheryl Spanier, Sheryl Spanier & Company

I hope this book, though quick to read, will encourage you to take time to reflect and get inspired about yourself. Look back on your past successes and create your new vision for the future.

Empowerment is very attainable for each of us as is the feeling of ownership and accomplishment.

If life seems overwhelming at times—remember Tom Watson, Sr., the former chairman of IBM, who knew how to inspire all 67,000 of his employees (and this was before e-mails, voice mails, and the technology we take for granted today). He carried index cards with him at all times upon which he wrote pertinent things about the people he met, their family, interests, etc., so he could always remember something personal and friendly to say to them. His kindness to his employees helped build IBM.

chapter 1

Networking Is a Mindset

Networking is a mindset—it is a strategy for life, a way to create connections that could last a lifetime and in all areas of your life. That is why I say networking is 24/7.

People come into your life for a reason, a season, or a lifetime. When you know which one it is, you will know what to do for that person. When someone is in your life for a *reason*, it is usually to meet a need you have expressed. They have come to assist you through a difficulty, to provide you with guidance and support, to aid you physically, emotionally, or spiritually. They may seem like a godsend and they are. They are there for the reason you need them to be. Then, without any wrongdoing on your part or at an inconvenient time, the relationship may come to an end. Sometimes they pass away. Sometimes they walk away. Sometimes they act up and force you to take a stand. What we must realize is that our need has been met, our desire fulfilled, their work is done.

1/ Networking Is Part of My Life

It is a mindset, not something that I *have* to do. I look at it as part of my make up. As I have told people in the past: Fake it until you make it or act as if it is. Just think: How can I be a resource to others, give something to them, or learn from them? When you keep those thoughts in mind and know that they are all part of strategic networking, it will become part of your life strategy and be with you all the time.

For instance, think right now:

⊙ Who can I send a note or article to that would help them?
⊙ What did I learn today from someone I know or someone I met or someone I observed? (By the way, we can also learn

from people we don't like or respect. They teach us what "not to do.")

⊙ To whom can you refer someone? Maybe you just spoke with a client or contact and they are looking for someone or you reach out for an exploratory meeting.

2/ Deliberate Networking Always (DNA)

When I say that networking is part of my DNA (Deliberate Networking Always), I mean that I look at how I give to others with the sheer passion of helping and being open. It is amazing how opportunities come back.

Paul Hansen is someone I met when I was giving a presentation to a group for another client friend of mine, Geoffrey Close whom I met through my dear friend Annmarie Woods (remember the chain of how people come into your life!). I had to be on a 6:01 a.m. train that is twenty minutes from my apartment, so you can see what time I had to leave my home. I got to the location that was an hour away for the early morning speech and there were only eight people in the room. However, my theory is that everyone knows at least two hundred people, so I was able to practice my presentation skills and also give my same message whether there were eight or eight hundred.

At the end of the meeting, Paul and I talked. He has since introduced me to twelve people and out of those twelve, I have been hired by five and am in talks with the others. I have in turn introduced him to several people and every day seems to bring another opportunity that might never have occurred if I had not spoken that morning.

So look at every opportunity as something larger than it appears. You never know and that is what makes it great. Also, make sure to you give every situation your best shot. Never wing anything—give your all.

3/ The ABC's of Networking

A Action, Attitude
B Belong to industry groups
C Call your Contacts, Connect
D Deliver what you say
E Empathy and Eye contact
F Friendly approach

G   Set Goals—"Go for it," Gratitude, Give
H   Humor and Help go Hand in Hand
I   Be Interested and have Integrity
J   Join and get involved
K   Keep in touch and be Kind
L   Listen, Learn
M   Motivate yourself
N   Niceness pays
O   Ask Open-ended questions, Opportunity
P   Practice—be Professional
Q   Set a Quota
R   Be a Resource and do your Research
S   Strategy and Smile
T   Timing is everything—Trust is key
U   Understand others
V   Be Versatile
W   Write letters
X   Do it with love XO XO, at least "like"
Y   Focus on "YOU," the other person
Z   Zeal for the possibilities of new and nurtured connections.

4/ Open Your Eyes—Networking Is All Around

Research tells us there are at least two hundred people who are already part of your network. Get reacquainted with them. Networking is about creating and developing opportunities through meeting and "connecting the dots" among the people you know. The following ten categories of people can be the beginning of a great networking success story:

1. Customers or clients—They are the lifeblood of your business. Build trustworthy and positive relationships.
2. Suppliers—Refer your supplier and improve your chances of staying on his/her radar screen.
3. Co-workers and colleagues—Office buddies are a powerful resource when networking. Invite a co-worker to lunch or coffee and get to know him/her better. Build your internal alliances.
4. People in your profession—Helping your competition can actually lead to greater opportunities to grow your business.

5. Former classmates—Seize the opportunities in your alumni magazine and pinpoint people who you might reconnect with.

6. Like-minded people—Expand your horizons. Extra curricular activities mean people with common interest and ambitions, or who share similar life experiences.

7. Neighbors—Turn a friendly wave into an invaluable conversation. Get to know your neighbors. You can open up the door for new opportunity.

8. Friends—Take time to nurture and cultivate your friends. Network with them in a positive way, never with expectations.

9. Family—They can be a great resource for networking opportunities. Think of how you can be helpful to those in your family.

10. People you meet by chance—Be kind to unfamiliar people. Airports, grocery store lines, and waiting rooms are filled with a world of networking opportunities. Keep your ears and eyes open. I learn something new every day by paying attention to the "universe."

Think of people you know who fit in each of these categories. The possibilities for networking are endless. Over time, as you build rapport and trust, these relationships lead to other contacts, partnerships, and opportunities.

5/ Think Motivation M. A. G. I. C.

M What the Mind can believe, the mind can achieve. It starts with your own self-talk. Be uplifting, be kind, and think about the best you have to offer. I once heard it said that depending on our self-talk, we are either in the "construction" or "destruction" business.

A Attitude is everything! It is our choice and sometimes a challenge to stay positive. When our personal "foundation" is good attitude, it lends strength on everything else we build on it.

G Set Goals and go for them. Keep your eye on a dream and work hard to achieve it. Write down your goals and keep them somewhere you will see them (like the mirror over the sink where you brush your teeth—at least twice a day!)

I   Have Integrity in all you do. A great reputation takes time to develop and can be destroyed in seconds. Honesty is the first word in the dictionary of virtues. You start by being true to yourself and making promises you know you will keep.

C   Care about others. Reach out to them. It is a sign of your inner strength, when you take the first step to help someone. Make someone else's life a little better—it comes back to you in ways unimaginable. That gratification is sure to life your spirit.

Take these steps to continually work a bit of "M.A.G.I.C." into your life:

1. Follow through and follow-up. Paul, another self-proclaimed introvert, ran into a high-powered exec at his global financial services firm. She suggested he stop by her office to catch-up. He did not think she was really serious and felt too shy and uncertain to pursue the opportunity. They ran into each other on another occasion. Again, she suggested he visit her office. Yet again he failed to visit and did not even send a thank you note because he did not want to appear intrusive or too pushy. Later at a meeting, she joined him and a colleague who raved about Paul's work. She replied, "Really? I can't seem get him on my calendar!!"

    This time, he took the cue, asked for her assistant's name and immediately scheduled a meeting. When they finally met, the meeting went well and they have continued a regular dialogue since. Now Paul is able to take his ideas to one of the highest levels of the firm.

What did he realize from this experience? Follow-up immediately, always send a thank you note, and do not "self negotiate" your way out of an opportunity to make a connection. This story also points out to me that you must always . . .

2. Have a goal and an action plan for every encounter—a huge advantage for someone with a nonstop networking mindset. You are prepared and you are ready to follow-up easily and efficiently. I leave my home every day with a specific goal

for meeting or nurturing my working network and for each meeting I have planned. I am then ready to follow up every chance encounter, as well as those I have planned in advance. Remember Lewis Carroll's dialogue in *The Adventures of Alice In Wonderland.* Alice said:

"Would you tell me, please, which way I ought to go from
    here?"
"That depends a good deal on where you want to get to,"
    said the Cat.
"I don't care much where," said Alice.
"Then it doesn't matter which way you go," said the Cat.

Or as I say: If you don't know where you are going, any road will take you there.

6/ Networking Becomes Natural

Networking is now "natural" to me. It was not always so, until I realized that networking is just a way of creating and maintaining good connections with people. Now I see the many opportunities that unfold when you have your ears, eyes, and mind open—just like a parachute. They all work better when they are open!

I think of each person I meet and each person I already know as a friend, client, prospect, or contact with someone else who could be one of these. A call came in one day from Carol who works for a large cosmetics company for which I had worked several years ago. She was referred by someone else whom I'd met briefly in a workshop. Carol explained that she was looking for a speech therapist to help her prepare for an important speech. I referred her to one I knew and also told her why I was not the specialist she needed. I sent her one of my networking books right away, and planned to call her after her big presentation to see how it went.

As life would have it, I was working at the same hotel where she had told me she was presenting and realized when I saw the company name that it must be her meeting. I took a chance, walked in, saw her nametag, and introduced myself! She was absolutely delighted to meet me, and she has now brought me into her management area. What did I do—took the initiative, was prepared, and followed up promptly.

7/ Opportunities Are Everywhere, or My Bras to Business Story

There I was shopping and the woman helping me said, "What do you do?" I gave her my "elevator intro for the general audience," and she said, "That is interesting. My friend is at (a large securities firm she named) and they are planning a conference." I followed up by sending a note and contacted two other people to be references, just in case. I got the assignment. Why? I followed up and I did so quickly. I also had my radar up—even though I was shopping.

Too often opportunities present themselves and we never take the action step.

Instead of saying to yourself, "I wish, I will, I want," you have to say: "Do it now, instead of tomorrow, which sometimes never comes.

Even if you feel like skipping that association meeting, for instance—GO. You just never know, and everyone you meet may already know someone you also know. At my Rotary Club luncheon, as an example, I sat next to a woman and we introduced ourselves. I asked her what she does and said, "I own a restaurant in New York." I asked her which one. "Marchi's," she replied. It sounded so familiar. Then I remembered, it was the restaurant owned by my dear neighbor Bernie's sister, Christine, a fellow Rotarian. So you just never know who might be sitting next to you.

8/ An Exercise in Attitude

Try this attitude exercise. Great client service requires us to be thoughtful and appreciative throughout the business development process. Clients do "assume" that you will thank them after you have done business. Here are a few "attitude of gratitude" thoughts to deliver in all your business relationships:

- ⊙ Go beyond surface information. Learn as much as you can about all your contacts and connections.
- ⊙ You must have "heart." People make decisions with their head and heart. Keep feelings in mind. It is the personal relationship that keeps you in good graces.
- ⊙ Give "thanks" for bad news as well as good. We usually celebrate successful deals and let clients know how much

their business means to us. Yet when we lose an order or a piece of business, we don't. We sometimes feel paralyzed by loss. Even with a rejection, show appreciation by sending a note of thanks for their time and consideration. You may be surprised by the outcome.

A couple of months ago, I got a new customer from floor duty. He wanted to purchase a condo in Tribeca. For our second viewings, I arranged to show him two properties late afternoon on a Friday. BOTH listing brokers failed to appear. (One got confused with his partner as to who was doing the showing, and the other got stuck in the subway for an hour.) Anyway, he was pretty upset, as was I. After thinking about it, I recalled we had stopped at his favorite little coffee place before our last viewings. I went over there, purchased a "coffee card," put it in a card with a note of apology, and delivered it to his building. He responded with an e-mail that thanked me for remembering where he likes to get his morning coffee, and we are still working on finding him the right Tribeca property.

—Deborah Fain, Associate Broker,
Prudential Douglas Elliman

9/ Act on Things Immediately

As an effective time manager, I act on things immediately because I know that tomorrow I will have ten more things I must do. Take things step by step, do what you say you will do, and as part of your brand you will be known for following up and following through.

10/ Managing Your Time

Get up ten minutes early—and be productive right away. You'll be surprised to discover how much time you have created through those extra minutes during which you can start a project or even connect via e-mail or handwritten note to people in your networks.

Ask yourself:
1. How much of my time is spent with customers or prospects?

2. Do I confirm appointments and plan my calls so they are closely clustered in a geographic area?

3. Is my paperwork done completely and correctly before I take it on my call?

4. Do I plan and practice my presentations and meetings?

5. Am I willing to meet with customers at their convenience instead of mine?

6. Do I frequently take non-productive coffee breaks and non-working lunches?

Help yourself:
1. List five ways in which you habitually waste time.

_____

_____

_____

_____

2. Explain how you could use your time more effective.

_____

_____

_____

_____

Don't get caught up in these Big Five Emotional Time Wasters: indecision, guilt, worry, perfectionism, and procrastination. Time is your best friend and also your biggest enemy. It keeps moving, so use it wisely. My friend says, "Sometimes you have to slow down to follow up properly. Don't multitask. When you do two things at once, you do neither well. Direct your attention and concentration to the moment and the task at hand. It will be hard at first, yet as you complete each thing, it will go faster and you won't have to stop and go back to correct the mistakes that happen when we try doing several things at once." Don't believe me— think of the last time you were on the phone and checking e-mail at the same time. Were you able to answer and respond to each task efficiently and with the attention it deserved? Also, when some-one stops into your office or meets with you—stop what you are doing and pay attention. Here is a tip—I always say, "How much time do we need right now?"

11/ Things To Do

Keep your to do list short and do them. You will have a sense of accomplishment. I keep a running log on my computer of things to do. Some will be put on hold so I can keep my daily to do list short and to the point.

Set chunks of time to do the tasks. Batch your e-mails and phone calls and even your note time. It is amazing what you can accomplish in only 10-15 minutes of productive time. I have known people who have mastered a new language by studying only 15 minutes a day consistently over time. Until you have done it, don't disbelieve it!

After two and a half years of belonging to a networking group and having no success, I attended an event to hear Jim Cramer speak. Sat next to a man from Denmark. After talking to him for awhile, I discovered that we had something in common. He was looking for an accountant for his new United States subsidiary of his Danish corporation, and I, of course, have cross border experience. He had an appointment later that week with a Big Four accounting firm. After further discussion, he agreed to come to my office and meet with me and my partner. After meeting with the Big 4 firm, I received an e-mail stating that he liked our firm better. Hence, a new client was borne!

—Joel Gensler, Eisner Accountants and Advisors

12/ Time Action Tips to Do Now

We make a living by what we get, we make a life by what we give.

—Winston Churchil

1.   Write daily, *specific, measurable outcomes* you want to achieve.

2. Every day review top projects and what can be done to move them closer to fruition.

3. Set your priorities—what is urgent and what needs to be done now.

4. Periodically, ask yourself, "Is what I am doing now the most important thing I can be doing at this time?"

5. Establish "place habits." Keep everything in a predetermined place.

6. Create systems for forms, checklists, and repetitive tasks.

7. Complete what you start. Leave nothing unfinished.

8. Plan—one hour of planning saves three hours of execution.

9. Develop a "do it now" approach. *Eliminate indecision.*

10. Pre-plan each week and allocate time to perform necessary functions.

11. At the end of each day, create a carry-over list of items that were not accomplished. Keep your time log and list going, so you can refer back to them.

12. Regularly analyze your use of time. Adapt and adjust when required to improve your efficiency and productivity.

13/ It's Not Who You Know—It's Who You Thank

While an entire industry has developed around motivating people through appreciation, it ultimately boils down to what our parents taught us: Say "thank you" to everyone. This may seem like simple etiquette, yet it is amazing what it can do for your business relationships. When we express our appreciation to clients, co-workers, and employees, their attitudes are positively affected, and positive attitudes impact business success.

An effective way to say "thank you" is with a gift. Not only is it an expression of gratitude, but it also serves as a reminder, keeping you in front of others so that they will contact you again. At the end of my training seminars and presentations, I like to stay in touch with the people who hired me and "signed the checks" for my work. One way I do that is to send a gift right after the program, and then follow up at least every three months with tokens of appreciation to keep my name in front of them.

One year, my holiday "thank you" gift to many of my clients and business friends was a glass shaped "light bulb" filled with mints, imprinted with, "A world of thanks," along with my name, phone number, and website. That gift showed others my appreciation while serving to promote my business, and it is something that people will use. I have seen it proudly displayed on people's desks. These kinds of gifts have a long shelf life because they can be refilled.

Other people require a more personalized thank you. In many cases, I take the time to find gifts that fit specific interests. For instance, I know that one client is a cat lover, so I found a wonderful crystal cat for him. To another client I gave an all-day spa treatment because she loves pampering. The point is to consider what people will appreciate most.

I was on AMTRAK on my way to Baltimore. Unusually, the train was crowded and someone sat down next to me. Soon we started chatting, and I found out he was on his way to Washington, DC. He told me he owns a business importing liquor, and I told him I was a director of a program assisting small business owners. As the conversation progressed he asked where I was from, and it turns out he imports cachaça from the same Brazilian state I'm originally from. We do all live in a very small world!

We exchanged business cards and soon he started sending me his newsletter, and letting me know when he was having tasting events. A month after we met, he sent me an e-mail with information about a show at Blue Note with a Brazilian singer I really like. I didn't tell him I was going, hoping to surprise him there, and I invited a friend to join me. The day before the show, I was hosting a networking event. The first person I had interviewed three years earlier for my online women in business magazine, showed up at the event. She owns three locations (a bar and two lounges) in New York City, and I told her about the cachaça importer I'd met a month earlier. She contacted him and started buying his products directly from him.

The story doesn't end there. The day of the show, he sent me an e-mail thanking me for the connection (I was not expecting anything in return, and was just happy to help both of them), and asking if I was going to Blue Note that night. I said yes, but my friend and I hadn't made a reservation, we were hoping to arrive early and see if we could get good seats. He immediately contacted the manager there, and arranged for us to have the best places in the house. We had an amazing time and as an additional bonus, the singer shook my hand! Networking on the train paid off in many ways.

—Elisa Balabram, womenandbiz.com

14/ Face Problems with Innovation

Exercise: Think Innovation when Facing a Problem

1.   Replace the word "problem" with the word "challenge" in your life.

2.   Define what the challenge is. (For instance, I have a prospect who keeps putting off our appointment.)

_____

3.   Prepare three suggestions to meet the challenge.

_____

4.   Write down what part of the challenge you can affect and what part you can't.

_____

5.   Prepare an action plan to meet the challenge. (For instance, I can change the place of the appointment and meet the prospect

for lunch; I can show up at the appointed time no matter what and say I forgot that he had changed it; I can show up unexpectedly and say I was in the neighborhood; I can put off the next appointment, putting the control in my hands.)

---

6.   Put the plan into action.

Life is a succession of moments. To live each one is to succeed.

—Coria Kent

chapter 2

Positioning Yourself— Your Brand YOU

As I sit in Starbucks and watch a city block of people clamoring in when there are three other coffee shops on the next block, I wonder why am I here. The coffee is strong and expensive, yet it is the aura or the mystique of the brand that brings me back. The other day when shopping at my favorite "local" Whole Foods, which is 34 city blocks from me, I considered why there are always droves of people there. Granted it is the customer experience of being there—great food, conveniently and creatively displayed, yet again the brand drew me in.

It reminds me of when I heard the founder of Jet Blue speaking at a conference. He talked about how they built their brand on flawless execution and taking care of the customer. Yes, I know they had a tough time in 2007 and they are also rebounding back. I fly Jet Blue all the time and after the troubles, I sent a copy of my second book to David Neeleman's office and said, "I am a stockholder and True Blue and I know you will be back to number one." The thing I admired most and have told many people—(networking)—is the next day I got a call from his office saying, "Thank you for the book and your continued support." So yes—I believe he is continuing to build his brand.

As he spoke at that conference some years ago, I heard someone say, "He came here to speak to this group for free." I thought about that comment. Here he was talking in front of a group of 200 executives about the airline's customer service, he gave everyone a Jet Blue cap, and he shared different stories based on his mantra of taking care of the customer. He was fabulous. Each person in that room was talking about his speech and Jet Blue when they left, praising it to everyone in sight. I know I did and am glad, by the way, that I have stock in each of these three brands! All the new business Jet Blue and Starbucks and Whole Foods get is from the buzz created and people telling each other . . . i.e., networking! So—did the CEO really speak for free!!!

15/ Your Brand Is Who You Are

Your brand is who you are and what people think about when they hear your name or think about you. Very much like the "customer experience" of life. It is not just how you look, it is how you "look" to others. It is painting in someone's mind a word picture of you—and how you create that image. For example, what do you envision from the following example.

My friend Vicky Amon is an amazing chef, though cooking is her hobby not her profession. When I asked her one night what she was preparing for dinner, instead of saying the plain and obvious, she said: "You could have 'fish, corn and salad' for dinner, OR, you could have pistachio encrusted tilapia, fresh corn on the cob with garlic/parsley butter, and a salad of Farmer's Market romaine, sliced avocado, Parmesan croutons, pine nuts and dried cranberries with a Dijon Caesar dressing." Which would you prefer? Again—it is all in the presentation and the articulation.

How would you create you? Think now about your own branding as you network. Here is how to get started:

1. Write down Your USPs—Unique Selling Points—we all have them.
2. Define what makes you "unique." In my case it is: "I follow up fast and efficiently." Your positioning strategy—how do you like to be positioned?
3. How do you "live" your brand? You must "walk your talk" so to speak.
4. What do people think of when they hear your name?

Put together your positioning statement and continually upgrade it. It should answer the following:

⊙ Who are you?
⊙ What business are you in? Or what business do you WANT to be in?
⊙ Who do you serve?
⊙ Who is your competition?
⊙ How do you differentiate yourself?

⊙ What unique benefit do you provide so that someone says: "He/she is the one for you on this project, job, etc."

Remember:
⊙ A position is how you are perceived in the minds of others.
⊙ A positioning statement expresses how you wish to be perceived.

16/ The Top 10 Cs of a Strong Personal Brand

1. **Correct**
   A strong personal brand is accurate. Authentic. So be true to yourself and your brand will shine.
2. **Concise**
   A strong personal brand can be described in one or two sentences. Distill your brand qualities into a brief statement that describes your unique promise of value.
3. **Clear**
   A strong personal brand is sure about what it is and what it is not. Make two lists describing what's on- and off-brand for you.
4. **Consistent**
   A strong personal brand is always the same. It is your promise of value to your customers, clients, managers, peers, etc.
5. **Constant**
   A strong personal brand is always there. Visible and available. It doesn't go into hiding.
6. **Compelling**
   A strong personal brand is appropriate and interesting to your target audience. It is relevant.
7. **Clever**
   A strong personal brand is highly differentiated and unique. It creates interest among your target market and separates you from others with similar skills and abilities.
8. **Connected**
   A strong personal brand is part of the appropriate communities. This means having a network of partners, colleagues, and customers.
9. **Committed**
   A strong personal brand is in it for the long haul.

10. **Current**

A strong personal brand is based in today with room to evolve for tomorrow. Be fresh and consistently updating.

17/ Your Personal Brand Statement—What People Think of When They Think of You

When you make your introduction to a new contact, does your Personal Brand Statement (PBS) meet these requirements:

1. **Hearing it makes people go "WOW!"** Providing good or excellent service is not enough these days. If you want to create a livelihood from your business (i.e., it's not just a hobby), then you need to stand out from the crowd. Clients are attracted to people who make them go "WOW!" Make what you say action-oriented and a benefit of what you do.

2. **Is only one breath long**. You should be able to say your personal brand statement in one "out breath." This is like creating a "sound bite" that people can easily remember. Test it: Can the other person repeat back to you what you said, verbatim? "I teach people how to create word of mouth advertising for themselves, their product, or their company."

3. **Clearly states practical benefits**. The practical benefit of what you are should be clear or at least clearly implied.

4. **Reflects your own personality**. Your PBS should be uniquely identifiable with you. If any one of your peers can say the same statement in the same way as you, then you need to inject more of you in it. Stay away from the generic, "I help you increase your profits." Your personality can be projected in how you phrase your statement, in the words you use, your tone of voice, etc.

5. **Projects confidence and energy**. Your PBS should roll off your tongue easily, without tripping. You must be able to project it.

6. **Gives enough to cause them to ask for more**. Your PBS is a "teaser" to start a dialogue with your customer.

7. **Fits with who you are—is real and grounded**. Going beyond reflecting your personality, your PBS basically describes how you express your personal mission in the physical world, your role in the world. Use "I" phrasing instead

of trying to create the impression that you're something bigger or other than who you are. (This is a tendency especially with self-employed people.)

8. **Can be made into an even shorter form**. Your PBS should be almost like a slogan, brand, or theme.

9. **Can change with time**. Your PBS evolves with time, reflecting what you are passionate about at the moment. You can continually change it.

10. **Can be repeated easily by others**. The ultimate success of a PBS is how well it creates "buzz" or word of mouth. If your PBS meets all of the above requirements, people will accurately talk about who you are and what you offer, triggering the attraction forces that work so well!

18/ Appearance Counts

Appearance certainly counts—it is about putting your best foot forward and no pun intended here. However, to make a more successful impression, here are four things I've learned you need to upgrade:

1. Your haircut/style (Anyone who knows me, will agree I do this constantly.)
2. Your shoes
3. Your watch
4. Your briefcase

We all notice things about someone. Also, wear your "signature style"—whatever yours is—just be sure to make it work for you, feel comfortable in it. The most important thing you ever wear is your smile, self image, and confidence.

19/ Your Personal Presentation

Your Presentation—we are "always presenting to someone":

1. Limit your own talking.
2. Listen to the other with your eyes and ears.
3. Ask open-ended questions.
4. Hold your thoughts—don't interrupt.
5. Use positive interjections.
6. Use persuasive, positive selling words.

20/ I Can't Hear You Because What I See Is Louder

We've been taught "never judge a book by its cover," yet we do! It may be unfair to judge someone in a matter of minutes—yet that is sometimes all we have. Although how we dress doesn't change how smart we are, or how thoughtful, it does affect other people's opinions of us. Moreover, these opinions can affect our career advancement. Start to use your image as a tool.

The Institute of Group Psychotherapy says: "Mainly one thinks of others as one did on the first meeting: initial impressions tend to be preserved."

Why do we preserve our first impressions? We don't like to be wrong, and we develop a mindset to confirm and substantiate our initial reaction and do not want to change. We see what we expect to see and filter out things that we don't want to see.

How people are treated often depends on the first impression they give to others. Life is one constant change. World events, fashion, and ideas always change—so we must learn to keep changing. This is why it is important to look at ourselves objectively and keep abreast of what is right and needs improvement about our appearance. We usually feel better about ourselves when we make an effort to look our very best and communicate in a way that puts us in the best possible light.

21/ The Power You Hold

The first thing anyone notices when you walk into a room is your image. Within the first three seconds that person has already sized you up. In the next four, they create all sorts of opinions, and statistics tell us that their first impressions are right 67 percent of the time.

Are they right about you?

- ⊙ How would you describe yourself?
- ⊙ Does your appearance communicate to others the message you want to convey?
- ⊙ How important is it to you to present a positive and professional image as you represent your company?
- ⊙ As you develop your communication skills and image, how might your career benefit?
- ⊙ In stressful situations, what happens to your image, your first impressions, and your professional presence?

⊙ What communication situations seem to make you uncomfortable? Public speaking, interviews, etc.?

The more objectively you think about and respond to these
questions, the more effectively you will be able to manage and
upgrade your personal and professional growth.

Here are some quick tips to keep in mind as you work past
your first impression to the second one which begins when you
start to talk with someone:

1. Be pleasant. Your smile is a great opener.
2. Talk and act confidently. Confidence inspires confidence.
3. Be truthful and sincere. It goes with confidence.
4. Be enthusiastic. It's contagious.

It's been said that the impression you make in 30 seconds can
impact and be more important than anything you do or say in the
next 30 minutes.

22/ Self Image

Always stay true to yourself—only compete with yourself—that
is enough. Set your goals high and achievable and strive for new
and better things as they relate to your life and business. Yet—
know what you can and will do to achieve what you set out to do.
This is where the work comes in and meets up with opportunity
and luck—which I say is laboring under correct knowledge.

Be who you are to yourself. Be creative and think how do I
maintain my individuality at the company or in my business?
Individuality is key—not "cookie cutter" mentality.

23/ Become the "Facilitator"—Introduce Others

Find a way to take on this role—my client John Ng is a master
at this. He walks around a company meeting and brings people
together. He knows something about each of them and their work
and the department or region. His persona is continually raised
and highlighted. As he would tell you, he is rather shy and introverted, yet he has pushed himself to learn more about people and
take on this project to also enhance his internal company networking. Has it worked—yes, he continually gets promoted! He is
amazing!

24/ A Quick Self-Introduction for Every Event

Depending on your audience, situation, and environment—you need to introduce yourself in different ways.

- ⊙ At an industry event, for instance, I might say: "I take the anxiety out of networking and public speaking skills." And then as someone looks at me, I turn to him or her and say, "and what do you do?"
- ⊙ They may have forgotten that they asked me what I do and just tell me what they do. I always find a way to connect the dots back to me.
- ⊙ If someone says, "I am an attorney at a large corporate firm," I might respond with: "I teach attorneys 'rainmaking' skills so that they can get their points across simply and persuasively and attain new business."

I strive to set goals and find new ways to describe what I do and the benefits to each person I connect with "after" I learn what they do. Does it always work? No, however it is great practice and we find ourselves in situations every day where we can test out new sound bites. Think of a way to introduce yourself at the deli, the health club, a new event, cocktail party, school meeting. Just don't say your title—at first—give the action and benefit grabbers of what you do.

25/ Always Improve and Refine Your Skills

How do I continually refine my skills, my surroundings—biggest room being the room for self-improvement? Strive for the next big thing.

I recently joined a new club to take clients to lunches and dinners and to provide a place for expanding my social network. I have also gotten involved in two other charitable associations. Not only do I feel that I am giving back to others, I am also enhancing my knowledge by meeting new people from whom I continually learn.

Whatever you do, find the opportunity to always be learning and observing others. Sometimes instead of reading a magazine, I look at other people to see what they are wearing, how they are putting themselves together, how they speak, and what trends they are discussing. It is almost like treating the world as a "book without borders"— as you write each page with your experiences.

26/ Change Your Scenery

This does not mean moving, it just means changing one thing about your routine or status quo. Get out of your networking comfort zone. Go somewhere different—take a day trip to a museum, volunteer at a hospital, take a class on something that intrigues you yet is not in your "core business" life. Observe and connect with the other people you meet along the way. You never know what you'll learn from each and every walk of life, yet you will be enriched for it and have more collections in your small talk networking tool kit.

27/ Start "Client-Telling"

Take five of your clients, contacts, or business friends or associates to lunch. Introduce each to the other and create connections for the pure synergy of having other bright and interesting people meet each other. What you invest in this "event" will come back to you many times over the years—with all types of surprising and interesting opportunities.

I always think of the people first and how they might learn something from the others there, then what they will contribute by being there. Whenever I do this, it is fun, extremely interactive, rewarding, and is a wonderful way for me to continually nurture my network.

28/ Words to Live By

Think of these as your daily mantras:

- ⊙ Feel you deserve the best.
- ⊙ Develop strong habits.
- ⊙ Get uncluttered and organized—streamline things.
- ⊙ Create your own rituals.

When my friend Bob Lamb was a new entrepreneur, in order to feel he was "totally at work," he made sure to get up early every morning, got dressed, and went to mass before starting his day. Now successful in his business, he still gets up and attends mass first thing in the morning and comes back to his office inspired and ready to go.

What is your routine and how do you prepare for each and every new day? What goals do you set and how do you measure them?

29/ Reinvent Yourself

Or as I often ask myself, "In the grocery store of life, why would someone pick you up off the crowded shelf—are you new and improved, repackaged? I am constantly reinventing my appearance—just look at how my hair has changed on each of my book's jackets!

One day I was at my health club, when I noticed an old acquaintance staring at me. "May I help you?" I asked.

She said, "No, it's just that you just look like Andrea Nierenberg, however her hair is longer and darker."

First I smiled and thought, "How did she know me and think that anyone else would (she works for a client company)? And then I said, "It is me—shorter and blonder!"

I keep up on trends and fashions and continually live by the adage, if you have not worn or used it in two years, you won't, and you will not miss it. Give it to your favorite charity and create more abundance in the world and more space in your home.

Reinvent yourself with a new hobby, interest, or passion. Take on a new project. Think it through and then start. Don't wait. The time will never be perfect and free to begin. Just start, take the plunge and keep upgrading, modifying, and inventing along the way.

Reinvention is like change: Many folks fear change. It can be both scary and exhilarating. Change is our only constant, however, so do something today a little different—reach out of your comfort zone and see new results and learning opportunities each step of the way.

30/ Re-think Everything You Do

Check and double check. More opportunities are ruined through careless mistakes or by trying to do too much at once without focus.

Create a checklist. I have different ones for events and work and constantly upgrade and refine them. Start simple—just have one. For example, say you are going to an industry event today:

- ⊙ Set a goal to meet and connect with two or three people.
- ⊙ Be specific. Write out your goal for the event or meeting.
- ⊙ Have your "elevator intro" so practiced that it rolls off your tongue—for that particular audience.

⊙ Have your tangible and intangible tool kits with you and ready to go, including the following:

  ⊙ The research you've done before the event
  ⊙ Eye contact—look at someone as if he or she is the only person there
  ⊙ Ears open and ready to LISTEN—turn off other "volume" in your head
  ⊙ Remember body language and check your appearance
  ⊙ Smile
  ⊙ Turn off all other equipment
  ⊙ Business cards handy?
  ⊙ Small paper and pen portfolio to write your notes?
  ⊙ Create a "small talk" notebook, which contains anecdotes to stimulate conversation
  ⊙ Breath mints/hand cream
  ⊙ Business card cases—one for yours and one for the ones you collect.

⊙ Pack your note cards/stationery with stamps so you are ready to write your thank you notes.

I pull this checklist out before every event. I always want to be 120 percent prepared. Our most important power is the power of thought.

Thoughts are seeds you'll reap what you sow.
                                        —Emmet Fox

31/ Your Image Collection

Imagine that a photo was taken of you every time you met another person during the day. Then put together a mental photo album of all of the pictures—your Image Collection. Ask yourself what you "see" with these questions:

⊙ Do I come across as articulate, persuasive, and sure of myself?
⊙ Do I appear trustworthy?
⊙ Do I have a "winning image?"!

Research tells us the following makes a favorable first impression:

- ⊙ Good listener
- ⊙ Good appearance
- ⊙ Commenting back to the person on something they said to show interest
- ⊙ Ability to create a rapport.

chapter 3

Creating Connections

Finding a new job is really all about networking—the formal kind of networking done through recruiters (or "headhunters" as those professionals are sometimes fondly known), or informal networking through friends. You never know when a chance encounter or simple introduction will lead to your next big career move.

I was able to do just this a number of years ago when I worked at the New York headquarters of a huge global advertising network. A friend at another agency called and asked if I'd be willing to meet a colleague whom he thought was terrific. He had no idea where it would lead but thought since we were both in human resources and personnel development positions, we'd have a lot in common. So, we met over a lovely lunch and were soon deep in conversation about the industry and its talent needs. I thought she'd be perfect for a new executive training position at my company that hadn't yet been announced to the outside world.

Sure enough, I introduced her internally and within a month she was hired. Seven years later, she's still there, totally stimulated by her work and has become an invaluable executive at the company. Her responsibilities involve all the things she loves to do but never thought she'd be able to find combined into one position. She says it's her dream job, and it never would have happened but for a chance introduction . . . informal networking at its finest!

—Victoria M. Amon, Building People Assets

32/ Be Curious

"Are you a sports fan?" I asked the man on the shuttle between Boston and New York. He was reading a book about the Yankees versus Red Sox—always a great conversation opener anywhere on the East Coast. I later ran out and bought the book myself and recommend having a book with you at all times that could be a conversation-starter. You never know . . . Be curious.

33/ Be Curious at Work

Walk by someone's office or cubicle and find something to comment on to start a conversation.

Be curious in life. When I see something that is interesting—a piece of jewelry, of course—I might say, "Tell me the story about your watch."

In fact, I did this recently with a new client contact who is an Indian in the diamond business. He was wearing the most amazing watch at breakfast and I asked him about it. It turns out that he "won" the watch by purchasing raffle tickets for a charity. "I'd never won anything before!" he said as we discussed the charity with which he is now deeply involved. It opened an entirely new area for our conversations and shared information. Now I am on the lookout for more information for him in my list of interests so that I can send it to him as a much appreciated way to stay on his radar screen.

What happened in this instance? First, I learned something new about him, then I got an education about his favorite charity, and finally I found a way to stay in touch with him by noting his interests and being alert for more information for him about those interests. When you ask people— even those you know well—about themselves, you find new things, topics, and interests to file away and share with them when "life presents them." That is why I always collect what I call "vital information." You never know when, how, and to whom you can pass it along and brighten their day.

Here is another example of how curiosity can start a conversation. Sitting on a crowded New York City bus, I noticed that the woman next to me had an unusual radio around her neck—just what I was looking for. So I asked her about it. She could have just stared at me or given me a quick nothing answer, yet she graciously told me about this particular radio and how it had been helpful to her and her staff during 9/11. She told me it was her day off as a senior attorney at a large media company, and she was riding the bus because she hadn't been able to get a car service or cab.

We decided to meet for lunch some time soon thereafter.

Though she did not have her business card with her, when she got off the bus I wrote down her information on one of my index cards and followed up a few days later. We have since become friends and business colleagues. You never know—reach out, be curious.

34/ Notice People and Things about Them

My client John tells how he was buying a sandwich in a deli and saw someone with a T-shirt that had some funny saying on it. He laughed and made a comment, and by the time they had gotten their orders they were exchanging cards, finding some synergy in their businesses, and have been referring each other to some sizable jobs ever since. John, by the way, is a self-proclaimed introvert and not one to talk to many. In this instance, however, he reached out of his comfort zone and has been rewarded many times over.

High Flying Connection

When I was 24 years old, after getting my masters degree in communications and working for a year in advertising, I decided to move from New York to Los Angeles to fulfill my dream of working in the TV business in Hollywood. I'd been an intern at NBC in NY while in college in 1986, and my vision was to work for NBC in LA—the network of Cosby, Family Ties, L.A. Law, *and many other hit shows.*

So, my parents drop me off at JFK, and after a teary farewell, I board my American Airlines flight to LA. I'm walking through first class on my way to my coach seat in the back of the plane—but who is this man blocking the aisle? He turns around to take his seat and I see that it is none other than Grant Tinker—the CEO of NBC! I just couldn't believe it.

Two hours, then three hours into the flight and I'm still debating with myself: Should I go talk to him; should I not? Will I be bothering him if I do; will I kick myself in regret forever if I don't? Three times I go up and peek my head through the first class curtain only to chicken out and return to my seat.

Finally, with less than an hour to go before landing, it's now or never and I somehow get up the courage to do it. I march down the aisle, stop and turn towards him, and start rambling off the words that I had been rehearsing and revising in my head for the past four hours: "Excuse me, Mr. Tinker. I hate to bother you but I was an intern at NBC last summer, and I am moving out to LA to try to get a job in the TV industry—hopefully for NBC!—and again I hate to bother you, but I was wondering if you just might have a minute to give me any advice that might help?" With that, he smiles, gets up from his big, cushy, first class aisle seat, moves over to the window seat, and says, "Sure, have a seat for a minute. What's your name?"

Long story short, the CEO of the number one TV network took five minutes of his time and attention to give some bits of advice to a young, aspiring job seeker. And though I ultimately didn't end up at NBC, I left that conversation with a feeling of hope, optimism, and confidence, knowing that I was making the right decision. And though I'm 99 percent sure that Mr. Tinker probably wouldn't even remember this interaction, the lessons of leadership he left me with—by his words and actions—I still carry with me more than 20 years later.

—Todd Cherches, Management/Leadership
Development, Consultant & Executive Coach, New York

35/ Show Others You Value Them

1. Use their name. Everyone likes to hear his/her name and to know that you are interested enough to remember it.
2. Acknowledge their presence. Something as simple as: "Good morning. How are you, Mary? I missed you at today's meeting," can be a way to show someone you are aware of her existence.
3. Remember small details about them. To them it is not small and is a huge connector.
4. Remember their—and if you are really good, the members of their family's—birthday, anniversary, graduation, or other significant occasion by sending a card, gift, or calling. People are often impressed when someone they don't know well remembers occasions that are special to them. I remember because I write and store all of this.

5. Let the person know you are available to help them in some way. Use your expertise to help others (within acceptable boundaries and parameters).

6. Be in the moment when speaking to them. This means listening closely to what is/is not said, as well as body language when face-to-face. Letting someone know you are truly in the moment when you speak with them can be manifested by small acknowledgements of their personality, work, hobby, etc.

7. Give proper credit. Giving credit where credit is due is important to valuing someone. It also raises your credibility in their eyes.

8. Be fair, regardless of their status or position. Treating someone fairly means enforcing the rules of civility for everyone all the time.

9. Be equitable. Playing favorites because it suits your agenda or circumstances is devaluating to the receiver and to observers. Everyone has importance and deserves respect.

Amy and I own several weeks of time-shares and have used them all over the world. While in Mazatlan two years ago, we met a lady who also lived in Montana. We struck up an acquaintance while photographing a beautiful sunset. She says that's what led her to contact me last week and begin a client relationship. She says she was so impressed when I focused the conversation on her during our photographing session and not on my work, what I did, or who I was. She determined then that someday she would call me to help her plan her finances for her retirement years.

Almost 100 percent of my business comes from referrals and most of those clients have become close acquaintances. I still have fewer than forty client relationships and plan to always have fewer than 100.

—Roger Lewis, Financial Advisor
Global Private Client Group

36/ F.A.C.E. Tip

Face-to-face connections are sometimes overshadowed by

technology. Make it a point to create "face" or personal time with your contacts. Here is what that means to me:

F   Be Friendly. When you start any interaction with strong eye contact, you automatically connect and rapport begins.

A   Adapt to the other's surroundings. Look around when in someone's office, you can learn a lot. Maybe you recognize a book you've read on their shelf, or you learn you are both tennis players. Use these and other shared interests as a conversation starter. A tip: Err on the side of being conservative. Don't say—"Is that your mother?" It could be his wife or sister!

C   Connect and think of questions that will help you understand the person better. Do some "prework" before the meeting. We all feel more comfortable with a person who seems to have a genuine interest in us and wants to build rapport and trust.

E   Know when to exit. Take the lead to finish the meeting and thank the person for their time. No one will fault you for ending a meeting early. Less is more and you may be invited back.

37/ Don't Waste Opportunities to Connect

Lost opportunity . . . I was having dinner at a new restaurant with my friend and former boss Rick Botthof in a suburb of Chicago. The manager came around to introduce himself and see how our dinner was. He asked if we were from the area. Rick said he was; I said I was visiting on business from New York. He immediately shifted his attention to Rick, trying to find out about his business and whether he would refer colleagues to the restaurant. He ignored me and the possibility that I might be the visiting president of a large company who could refer my sizeable Chicago staff to his restaurant, or that I might be addressing more than 500 people from the area on business development and creating relationships the next day—which I was. What a mistake on his part!

To add fuel to the fire, before he walked away, he gave Rick his card and said to him, but not me, "Feel free to call me." If he had been smart and truly interested in business development, he would have taken both of our cards and then dropped each of us a note, saying, "Thank you for your visit, hope you enjoyed it and please come back." We would both have recommended his restaurant had he made this small gesture. Instead, I won't mention its name. No buzz created from this neglected patron, though the food was fine.

> *I wanted to let you know that since we met back at Deutsche Bank, I have read your book, and liked it so much that I purchased it as a gift for someone I mentored. She then networked her way to an exciting job on Wall Street. I am currently a second year MBA student at Stanford and in the process of figuring out what direction to go in my career. Your advice and techniques have been invaluable and I have made many of them truly mine and part of my everyday life.*
> —Jason Peter Torres, Stanford University

38/ Never Assume

We know what happens when we do. This is another reason I believe in biting my tongue and waiting before speaking. You could lose a sale, talk yourself out of something already sold, or make a fool of yourself.

One day I called information at the New York/New Jersey area bus transit authority. When the operator connected me, she said: "Good luck." Surprised, I asked her why, and she said: "Aren't you going to Atlantic City to gamble??" This was the furthest thing from my mind. I was going to speak at a financial services conference (could there be some similarity here?) Now I never go to Atlantic City without thinking of the assumption the operator made and how I could have been offended. Better to hold your tongue.

39/ Learn by Listening—and Don't Talk Just to Talk

A man I respect told me his philosophy about the power of the tongue. He cites a passage in the New Testament which described the effect of our little tongues on our lives. He tells the story this way:

> *Take ships for example. Although they are so large and are driven by strong winds, they are steered where the pilot wants to go by a very small rudder. Likewise the tongue is a*

*small part of the body, but makes great boasts. Consider
what a great forest is set on fire by a small spark.*

Think of this before saying something without considering the
repercussions of what and how it will affect someone else. We can
all go to school on this very thought each and every day of our
lives and learn valuable lessons about creating a better and sweeter
environment—with thoughtful tongues.

40/ Become a Better Listener

The Talmud says "the highest form of wisdom is kindness."
Sometimes the kindest thing you can do for someone who is
troubled is to listen. Death and life are in the power of the tongue–
–just reading this gives me goose bumps.

Better Listening

- ⊙ Force yourself to ask questions.
- ⊙ Slow down your "thinking rate." We think at 500 words a
  minute and talk at 150. That's why our minds wander.
  Stay focused.
- ⊙ Listen for the theme. Get the key issues.
- ⊙ Use key words as memory aids. Identify key words and
  use them as memory stimulators. For example—something
  you remember easily, like where they are from or where
  they work.
- ⊙ Rearrange the information that you hear. Organize it in a
  way that is logical for you.
- ⊙ Take notes: You talk to so many people, you have to write
  things down to remember them all.
- ⊙ Keep refining your skills. These tools and techniques may
  sound simple, but the challenge is in the execution.
- ⊙ Create value with every contact, and your business will
  live forever, says my friend Bill.

41/ Remembering Names

Remembering names is hard, especially at a trade show where
you're meeting many people at once. Here are some easy steps for
remembering:

1. When you meet someone look him or her in the eye and
   keep your eye contact while you are talking.

2. When they mention their name, repeat it out loud, "Hi, Tom, it's great to meet you." (What you're doing is making them feel good by using their name and it's also going into your memory bank through repetition. It also forces you to really listen. Just mention their name once or twice—not more.

3. Form some type of association about them. Maybe they have the same name as a friend, or their name rhymes with something. Whatever, we remember in pictures and this will help our mind paint a word picture.

4. Erase this phrase from your mind: "I'm no good at remembering names." Replace it with: "I'm getting better at remembering names." What the mind hears internally, it remembers.

42/ If You Put Your Foot in Your Mouth, Make Sure You Are Wearing Nice Shoes!!

What a reminder to me! We have all done it and yet, be so careful to "bite your tongue" the next time you even think it could be in error.

I was speaking to a group of people and happened to mention the name of someone I had worked with. Even though I was saying something nice, I realized that it is never a good idea to name drop. To make the matter worse in my mind, I asked the group if anyone knew this person. When I thought about it later, I realized I probably offended some people and in the future I would "zip it" when it comes to mentioning specific names unless I have total permission to do so!

43/ Create Great Connections Between Your Contacts.

Think of those you like, trust, know, and respect. Who among them might have synergy? Ask those with potential connections for permission first, then take the action step of introducing them by note, e-mail, or telephone call. Then step away and let them take the next steps. Never keep score. Do it for the sake of expanding the networks and referral and relationship sources of your owned valued contacts. One person told me he heard that "making connections is like a chess game." He likes thinking of who would be good to know each other and he bases it purely on trust, respect, and possible synergy.

A client of mine was interviewing for a job at the company of another client. Both clients were very close friends and although they did not know each other, I knew that they would align both personally and professionally. They were both intelligent, kind, and passionate.

I reached out to the client at the prospective company, Client A and asked her to put in a good word for Client B. She did so and sent a lovely note that raved about me and said that any person about whom I raved was good enough to work at their company. The e-mail was extensive and elaborate and glowing. It went to the senior most person doing the interviewing.

Client B did interview and ultimately received the job. She felt that the e-mail from Client A helped enormously. I was then moved off of both businesses to take on a new assignment prior to Client B's start date. Client A and Client B became friends professionally and personally—they adored and raved about each other from the instant they met. They felt as though they were friends before they started which led to terrific collaboration on the businesses.

When I was moved back onto Client A's business, they both became my clients again and we still live happily ever after today.

We call it our sorority.

— JoAnn Accarino, ZenithOptimedia

44/ Before You Contact Someone to Whom You've Been Referred, Check with the Person Who Referred You

If you've learned something personal about a person to whom you've been referred by the person who referred you, you'll have a much more gracious way to engage him or her in conversation. Besides, you'll be making two people feel great at the onset—the new person you are connecting with and the person who referred you!

45/ Random Acts of Kindness

Besides feeling great and being a good person, do something kind—just to do it. Here are some things I like to do:

⊙ When you pay your toll at the toll booth, pay for the person behind you.

- ⊙ When you get on the city bus, pay for the person behind you who looks like they are having a bad day.
- ⊙ Just don't let the recipients of your kindness know it came from you. The point is to do it just to make someone else feel good—and as a surprise.

One time, I was having lunch with my friend Jon Lambert when we saw a group of soldiers who were on leave and having some sort of a gathering. Before we left our meal, Jon said to the manager, "I would like to pay for all of them, but don't tell them, please." There were 25!! When we were leaving, however, the soldiers caught up with us. The smiles, hugs, and pure gratitude were, as my friend Jon said, "worth their total weight in gold and many times the cost of the lunch!"

Another time, as I was leaving the hairdressers, it started pouring down rain. I always carry an umbrella with me, but the woman next to me didn't have one and had to get to a meeting. I turned to her as I was walking to my car and said, "Here you go, and you can give it to someone else when they need an umbrella!!"

Make someone feel good and it comes back to you!

46/ Clothes Make the Opportunity

Walking into a cocktail party I saw a very powerful Wall Street executive who was wearing the same St. John outfit that I was. I walked over to her and said, "Excuse me, I want to compliment you on your incredible taste in clothes!" She responded by saying how much she appreciated my sense of humor! After the event, I sent her a note and the card of Don Klein, my great personal salesperson at the boutique if she was ever interested.

Net(working) result—the boutique got some new business, and Don was so happy, I now get invited to more of their store events and I also landed a piece of business from the executive.

So—ladies, if you are ever wearing the same outfit or even same designer as another person at an event, don't despair, turn it into an opportunity to connect.

47/ Networking Domino Effect

I met my friend Scott Swendenburg at a conference, stayed in touch, introduced him to a group as a speaker, then to a radio show, and now he is writing his own book. From one person to another—just being nice. Keep the process going with your friends and contacts.

48/ Say Thank You—Even if You Didn't Get the Business

Next time you might!

49/ Re-connect with Four People a Week

This week call a client or prospect you've been out of touch with—a former business colleague, a friend from the past, and a current friend you haven't spoken with for a while. Catch up, up-date your notes, and be ready to do some new business.

50/ Who Would You Like to Meet?

Make a list of key people you'd like to meet in your industry or profession. Determine what organizations, places, and people they know and find ways to connect with them. Call or connect with someone you do know and ask if they would write a letter on your behalf and offer to save them the work by writing it first and ask-ing for their comments and edits.

If you can conceive it, you can achieve it.

51/ Join Civic, Industry, and Professional Groups

Research and join a civic, industry, advocacy, or professional group. Go to two meetings, meet two people, and set up two fol-low-up meetings—before you make your decision to join. This is my "2-2-2 Strategy." It works every time. My theory: It is quality—not quantity that counts.

Join for the sake of giving, not getting. You will get a lot back over time. Write down now a couple groups you are interested in and make the call to get started. Once you are in a group, volun-teer, write an article, or join a committee. Take the action to be-come known in your organizations of choice. Results will happen.

52/ Change the Way You Look at Things

When you change the way you look at things, the things you look at change—Wayne Dyer said this and it is engraved in my mind—think forward and think positive.

53/ Follow Your Interests

Take a class, join a health club, or go on a different type of vacation. I have now gone on African safaris, and trips to Russia and India. Be adventurous in your own way. Remember, you need like-minded people in your network. Bonds will develop and create connections that you otherwise may not have made. From my African adventure, I met a woman who was extremely successful in California. She suggested I join the Rotary Club. At first I put her suggestion on hold because I felt I belonged to too many things. However, as life would have it, I was asked to speak at the local Rotary. I did join and have made amazing friends and contacts in a short time. Again—change your perception and do it.

54/ Action Tips to Think About

Think about the people you come across in meetings, sales calls, or in a registration line at trade shows. Everyone has the potential to be an important contact. More importantly, the golden rule is: Instead of looking at networking as getting something from others, think of how you can be a resource for those people and what you can learn.

Get out your hoe and seed bag. Here are some tactics that will help you yield a bountiful harvest in the future:

- ⊙ Become aware of your environment. Learn by emulating successful networkers around you. Identify what they do that appeals to you. Your environment also includes what you read. From now on, look at the newspaper with a "networking" eye, and listen to the news with a "networking" ear. When someone interests you, send a note that compliments him or her.
- ⊙ Be results-oriented and have a plan. Make networking a part of your daily routine. For example, if you're off to an association meeting, set a goal to make two new contacts and then follow up with them. Following up is the most crucial part of the process. It separates the pros from the amateurs. If you think it's time consuming to develop a relationship with the new people you meet, you're right. You'll never know in advance which "lead" will turn out to be productive unless you take the time and effort to find out.
- ⊙ Find an original approach. For example, with my business, I have an easy-to-read newsletter that I e-mail to customers, prospects, and friends. It is also mailed to people I

meet at trade shows. Take the initiative and be the one to make the first move. The person who hesitates is lost.

⊙ Be a joiner and get involved. Sitting on the sidelines won't get you noticed. Have an active life. I recently joined a business club where I can entertain clients and enhance my own network. I immediately wrote a letter to the president of the club, and asked him how I could get involved with some of the committees. He called me back and the first thing he said was, "I like your direct approach." My networking did not stop with him; I also became friendly with the support people there, remembering them with a note of appreciation. Think about the business organizations in which you can actively participate.

⊙ Perception is reality. People remember what they see and hear from you. Make a good first impression that never stops impressing others. Treat new contacts with special care and importance. Reintroduce yourself to those individuals who are still getting to know you.

⊙ Have measurable tactics. Every good strategy has specific action steps that can be monitored. For example, each week call three people you haven't spoken to in 90 days. Keep a log of contacts along with the type of follow-up you used. Decide which approaches are working best for you. While you can scientifically measure results, remember that networking is an art form expressed by you.

We are continually faced by great opportunities brilliantly disguised as insolvable problems.

—Lee Iacocca

This section gave you more food for thought in business, life, and making and creating connections. Act on one right now.

chapter 4

Building
Relationships

55/Getting to Know Your Contacts

Here is my list of information to know about your contacts, clients and prospects as you get to know them. Some are obvious and some only develop over time as the relationship grows—and it will as you listen and record and find out new information about them.

Here we go—and keep adding to it:

Name _____

Company _____

Phones: Company _____

             Home _____

             Cell _____

Address _____

_____

Birthday _____

Hobbies/Interests _____

_____

Favorite foods _____

Favorite restaurants _____

_____

Vacation interests _____

Spouse name _____

Kids' names _____

_____

Pets _____

Preferred method of communication _____

College and/or grad school _____

Special holidays _____

continued on next page

continued from previous page

Job promotions/moves _____

_____

Who you refer to them _____

Whom they refer to you _____

How you met and when _____

Likes   _____

Dislikes   _____

Previous job _____

Anniversary of doing business together_____

Professional organizations _____

_____

Assistant's name _____

What "motivates" them _____

_____

Their advice to you and information given to them

_____

_____

How you have handled any problems that have arisen
    with their account _____

_____

What they said when you ask them: "Why do you work
    with me?" _____

_____

When is their "busiest" season for work, i.e., accountants
    during tax time or when they are in planning if they
    are in media _____

_____

What keeps them "up at night" on work projects? _____

_____

What you have learned that will interest them in your re-
    search about their work or industry?_____

_____

Bonus tip to ask yourself: This person calls me when (fill
    in the blank) _____

Then to the same for when you connect with them: why,
    for what, etc. _____

_____

56/ Clients For Life

Think this way starting now. In today's competitive world, we need to be proactive about maintaining and improving relationships with our existing clients. As we do this in genuine ways, we deepen the ties we have as associates in business *and* as fellow travelers. Here are some ways to further these relationships (and remember—some of your "clients" can be your internal co-workers or business units within your organization):

Client Retention

1. **Spend thirty minutes each day talking with two existing clients.** Ask them what they want, what they need, and what they like/don't like. Implement the ideas that work for you.

2. **Invite your "champion clients" to serve on your board of directors.** Your clients will add wisdom and will know that you value their judgment.

3. **Post newspaper/magazine articles about your clients' achievements in your establishment.** People love to be acknowledged for their wins. A classic picture frame will add an elegant touch.

4. **Invite clients/customers to test a new product or service before you offer it to the public.** Your customers will have insight about what the public wants. This will save you energy and will send the message to your client that they are the first to experience something new.

5. **Partner with your clients in a marketing effort, workshop, or special event.** The more opportunities you have to spend with your clients, the more you will connect on a personal basis.

6. **Provide value every day.** Freebies and discounts are a great way to keep clients and make new ones. Gifts like a free car wash, haircut, facial, or gift certificate are always popular. Offer something unique to show your customers that you are creative and open to new ideas.

7. **Follow the successes of companies that have a reputation for outstanding customer service.** By learning from the pros, your business will grow and improve.

8. **Connect with your clients through common interests.** Find out what you share in common with your clients. They

will remember you and develop a sense of friendship.

9. **Spend time with your competition, and know what they are doing.** In this competitive world, it is difficult to stay ahead. Design a suggestion box for customers to let you know about better prices and better service.

10. **Remember! Your customers are always right even if they're wrong.** Thank your customers for both positive and negative comments. Do all in your power to make them happy.

Keep these in mind everyday with clients and contacts.

57/ From Complaint to Opportunity

1. Listen to the customer's complaint.
2. Take complaints seriously and act fast.
3. Empower everyone in your organization to handle complaints.
4. Be proud to be associated with your company.
5. Avoid focusing on or affixing the blame.
6. Let the customer suggest alternatives.
7. Minimize the time between a complaint and when it is resolved.
8. Trust in the customer's sincerity.
9. Empathize with the customer.

58/ People You Need in Your Network

You can learn something from almost everybody with whom you come into contact in your life—a benefit both professionally and personally. People you meet may also know others who can help you. An important first step to expanding your "worldwide web" is to identify the people with whom you want to build relationships. As described in chapter 1, the types of people you need in your network include:

⊙ Customers or clients
⊙ Suppliers
⊙ Neighbors
⊙ Like-minded people

- People you meet by chance
- Friends
- Family

Write down the names of people you know in each of these categories who would either take or return your phone call. Then think of a specific reason why you should contact them. For example, if you know that your neighbor is a real estate agent, tell him or her about an article you saw in the paper about trends in property values. The point is to find a meaningful way to connect with people that will benefit them.

59/ It's All about Your Client

Finding clients and nurturing them is one key ingredient to success. Each of these people can become an advocate to help you grow your business. Satisfied clients, business contacts, friends, and your team, can be your best sales and marketing champions because they know and respect you. Here are some ways to earn the trust of your clients, both internal and external, and stay on their radar screens:

- **Befriend your client**: Break bread with them or take them to an event. Develop a relationship with your client as you would with a friend. They often do become one.
- **Provide dazzling service**: Credibility is everything. Provide top service and always go the extra mile.
- **Place their needs first**: Be proactive. Find ways to make their life and work easier and more productive.
- **Be their advocate**: Make connections for them. Help them find new business, a valuable connection, or anything that enhances their life or solves a problem.
- **Refrain from keeping score**: Do it because you like and respect them. When you show that they're always on your radar screen, you'll find yourself on theirs as well.
- **Keep giving your clients added value**: Increase your services to them. In addition to what you are already doing, send them a new suggestion, idea, strategy, or a tip of the month (or week) that will help grow their business.

Using these strategies, you will earn your clients' trust and respect over time and will see the results in a solid network of contacts. They will become your advocates and talk about you and your business in a positive way. This is a credibility factor that comes from working hard and smart to create powerful connections.

Networking Gail Style

My mantra is: Work should be a by-product of having fun. By that, I don't mean to be glib or imply that I don't take my work seriously—far from it. There is a serious purpose to my work in professional fundraising. I have found that by creating fun, one attracts success both in developing and retaining donor and professional advisor relationships. And I've noticed a direct correlation between having fun and an increase in the number and amount of planned gifts. This is accomplished by planning and maintaining periodic intimate, casual networking events. These events benefit others as much or more than they do me. That is the best thing, as far as I'm concerned.

An example is a group of advisors and donor prospects who meet for appetizers and cocktails at a trendy rooftop restaurant locally every month to six weeks. The advisors are from different disciplines so they are able to find ways to do business together, as well as develop business relationships with the donor prospects. Each time something different is celebrated—a birthday, a promotion, a Wednesday—it doesn't matter. New people are added to keep things fresh. There is always a reason to get together. The fallout from all this fun includes a deepened trust and bonding that transcends business relationship. The donor prospects and advisors become friends and the business "just happens" . . . in abundance.

—Gail Robson, Planned Giving Director,
American Cancer Society

60/ Ways to Sharpen Your Business Edge

⊙ **Pay attention to articles in newspapers, magazines, and television shows about trends and changes in national and international demographics.** This information can be very helpful in finding new business opportunities for you, increasing profits and ideas for providing additional value and service for people who do business with you.

⊙ **A marketing plan is only as good as the tracking system you put in place.** It will enable you to see where your dollars are being the most beneficial to your business. Track each client or request for additional information. Get in the habit of asking your clients, "How did you hear about us?" Then keep that information in your database along with their name, address, and any special request or preferences they may have.

⊙ **It is important to know how that client found you—and to thank that person or source—(more business will come from it).** You will see patterns begin to emerge that will help you focus your marketing efforts where they are the most effective.

⊙ **Joining your local Chamber of Commerce and/or other trade associations will give you more places to network and connect with other small business owners.** You will be able to share experiences and bounce new ideas off of these people. At the same time, you can share your experiences and solutions to problems they may be facing. More and more, the business world works best when businesses co-partner and act in a mutually interdependent way.

⊙ **You are always marketing your business and yourself.** Even if you don't think you are in a "business setting," you are still conveying an impression of yourself and your business. Be helpful and listen to people. Helping people is rewarding all by itself, but you will find that other people notice and will think of your business first when they need the product or service you offer. They'll know you are committed to the community and to helping others because you helped them.

⊙ **When advertising, don't think big, as in circulation and exposure—think targeted**. Find out how your clients spend their time, what they read, and what they like to do for fun. Then use this information to help you target your marketing efforts so your message will directly reach the people who are interested in your product or service.

- ⊙ **Develop different ways for potential clients to get to know you**. Writing articles, doing workshops, or speaking are great ways to interact with your potential customers. They will get to meet you and experience your style first hand. If you are uncomfortable doing these things, think of ways to start small and build your confidence. Find a way to give a presentation at your local bookstore or library on a book you found interesting that has some correlation to the services you provide. Perhaps you could partner with someone else and present together.

- ⊙ **Be consistent in your communications**. What is most important to you? What is the essence of what you provide to your clients that is fulfilling to you? Narrowing your focus and determining what you want to share will help you define your business style. You can then have all of your marketing materials reflect that style. This will attract the best clients for you.

- ⊙ **Help people find "doable" ways to start and then to continue to work with you**. Think of ways you can tailor your services to smaller businesses or organizations so they can begin working with you on a limited way and grow into more services or products. Offer different services with different price points. People like to test things out, make sure they feel comfortable and pleased with the services you provide. Let them experience first hand the value you provide and want to continue to do more business with you.

- ⊙ **Define the kinds of client projects or goals that you would enjoy working with most**. Are there clients in a particular industry, age group, personal philosophy, or with a greater level of challenge that you would like to work with? When you focus on the kinds of clients and projects important to you, you will attract those most rewarding for you to work with. You'll be excited by the work you do together and have a great person to refer you to other potential clients with these qualities. Go where they go, read what they read, start to integrate yourself.

61/ The First Call Is the Beginning of Many

Follow up with cards, notes, gifts, get-togethers. Find opportunities to stay on your contacts' "radar screen." Focus on tuning into the radio station MMFI-AM—"Make Me (the other person) Feel

Important About Myself." Stay in touch, learn about them, and make connections that will be helpful in their life. Here are five convenient ways to remain connected to your business contacts:

- ⊙ **Handwritten notes:** Send a personal note in the form of a "FYI" (For Your Information), "Congratulations!" "Nice talking to (or meeting you)," "Thinking of you," or "Thought you would be interested." Since handwritten notes are becoming rare, the ones you write will make an impression.

- ⊙ **Holiday cards:** Seasons greetings and special occasion cards let your contacts know you care about what's special to them. Consider the profile and interests of your contact when sending a card. Your recipients will continue to be surprised and happy to hear from you.

- ⊙ **Interesting e-mails:** A creative e-mail with a message tailored to your recipient can also make you stand out. Forward interesting online articles and Web sites, inspirational quotes, pictures, videos, or a monthly tip. Personalize your e-mails with a friendly note or signature and keep your contact's needs in mind.

- ⊙ **Your newsletter or article:** Send your contacts your own published articles or create one if you have yet to do so. Compile your articles in a newsletter with tips and techniques that can help advance their business. Write a personal note with each article or newsletter to grow and keep these relationships. With an e-newsletter, personalize it— every software program enables you to do this.

- ⊙ **Gifts:** Sending a nice gift sets you apart and shows your contacts you appreciate them. Whether sending food, flowers, or a book, be sure to consider your recipient's preferences and habits. Send a gift that can be shared with others in the company. Do what works for you and makes your client happy, and remember keep it professional. And think, "How would I react getting this particular gift." Think it through—one size does not fit all.

Think of staying in touch as proactive, and as a nice way to nurture your network regularly. When the opportunity arises to ask for some advice, you can do it easily because you have built a solid relationship.

62/ A Simple Note Goes a Long Way

Successful networking means an effective follow-up strategy for building your contacts, connections, and trusted advisors. After any meeting, it is important to connect with your new contacts and follow up with your friends or acquaintances to nurture them. Because timing is of the essence, be sure to follow up quickly, efficiently, and genuinely. It is the key to growing your network and business.

The following are the four "Must-Dos" after a meeting:

1. **Generate a greeting:** Within twenty-four hours after a meeting, send a note, e-mail, or call to let your new contacts know how much you appreciated getting to know them. Doing this distinguishes you and you stand out. I am still amazed how often this is not done.

2. **Present your promise:** When you promised to send materials, call to set up a meeting, or give a referral, keep your word. Following up in a timely manner will establish you as a trustworthy person. Under-promise and over-deliver.

3. **Dial the digits:** Within two weeks after suggesting a get-together, call your new contact and set up lunch or a more formal meeting. Always send a courtesy e-mail or call to confirm the day before. Your sincerity and professionalism will shine through.

4. **Give the gift of thanks:** When a contact provides you with a referral or offers to pass your information along, be sure to say thank you and keep him or her in the loop by letting them know the developments and results that occur. These simple gestures of appreciation go a long way when building your network.

These follow-up acts are purely common courtesy and professionalism. They help build solid relationships for the future, and show respect for others. "Respect" is the key word. Remember, people do business with those whom they know, respect, and often like.

After a recent networking meeting, there was a giant line to meet the speaker, Martin Everette, Director of Affirmative Action at many NYC Hospitals. Seeing that I would be at the end of such a long line of anxious entrepreneurs, and seeing how tired he looked, I walked up to him and simply asked for his card and told him I would like to write him later on since he was so busy now. He looked so honestly tired. He laughed and said, "Thank you, I am," and gave me his card.

That day I wrote him a personal note and a small intro about my company. He called the day he received it, and said he loved my letter and how much he appreciated my not joining the long line. He set up a meeting to meet my boss and introduced her to a few other people and gave her great leads and his personal recommendation! That led to us connecting with a lead and being given the chance to bid on a small promotion. After we won it, they gave us a chance at a sizable order and we won that and a great relationship with them that keeps growing with mutual respect. All because I wrote a warm follow-up. You never know.

—Joyce Ellen Kuras, Director of Procurements,
Advantage Printing Inc.

63/ Develop Advocates

Who is your advocate? Your clients can be. In business, networking is a necessary skill for finding and developing new clients and keeping those you have. It's also an opportunity to create advocates for your business. These advocates will be your best sales and marketing champions because they know and respect you. Here are some potential advocates you might consider:

- ⊙ **The satisfied client:** Where else could you find a better advocate? Though you may feel awkward asking for referrals, there are ways to make asking easier. For instance, ask for feedback after you have provided a product or service. Then if it's positive, suggest you would be "happy to work with anyone else whom they could recommend."
- ⊙ **Your team:** Everyone from the bottom up should be responsible for selling your company. Smart networkers know to build relationships and alliances with those who are not only above them organizationally, and also down, sideways, and across. This is a key point. Keep in touch with receptionists, office administrative people, and those in other departments to stay informed of leads they may develop for you.

- ⊙ **Colleagues in business:** In today's specialized world, many of the contacts you make in your industry will refer business to you because you specialize in an area that is needed. Fine tune a 20-second "infomercial" about your services or products that will "stick" with people long after the conversation has concluded. More on this at the end of this tip section. Think how you can be of help to them and what you can learn.
- ⊙ **Friends and neighbors:** We work hard at building friendships based on mutual trust and respect. As you find out more about your friends' and neighbors' work, you'll want to help them, and over time, they will most likely want to help you if they can. Always put the relationship first when networking with personal connections. Yet, always be aware that opportunities come up in places you may least expect!

Of course, even when we've made advocates, we still need to sell ourselves directly to prospects and clients. When our advocates open the door for us, we must stay in there and close the deal. The more advocates believe in us, the more convincing they'll be with new clients. Make a list of your advocates and get a plan together to cultivate these relationships starting today!

64/ What Do You Do—Your 20-Second Infomercial

The most commonly asked question at networking events is, "What do you do?" How you respond can be the beginning of a great business relationship. You must be prepared to answer this question in a clear, concise, enthusiastic, and memorable way—all in 20 seconds or less! This statement is called your 20-second infomercial or "hook" or "grabber." Here are some questions to help you determine whether your personal introduction is effectively communicating who you are:

- ⊙ **Does my opening statement make the other person say, "Tell me more?"** Your statement needs to leave your contact eager to find out more about who you are. Offer a brief and exciting description of how you serve or help people.
- ⊙ **Am I specific enough?** Make yourself stand out. Be sure to paint a word picture in the other person's mind that is easy to visualize.

- ⊙ **Do I enjoy what I do and does it show?** Come across as enthusiastic and upbeat. When you're excited about your work or professional interests, you naturally come across as an energetic and passionate person.
- ⊙ **What benefits and solutions to problems do I provide?** Offer yourself as a problem solver. Always think of how you convey what you do as a benefit to the other person or a solution to a problem.
- ⊙ **What makes me and my services unique?** Distinguish yourself from the competition. Your grabber has to convey your exclusivity and the service you provide. Your personal introduction statement has to be particularly appealing when meeting someone for the first time. When preparing it, think about how you want to be remembered, what will make you stand out, show your uniqueness.

Think of several different introductions, based on each audience, group, market you serve—the list goes on. Keep coming up with different and unique and innovative ways to describe "who you are."

65/Gratitude–and Your Attitude

Always say thank you. Thank you! Thank you! Thank You! You can't say it enough with sincerity.

Take time every day to say thank you to those who have contributed to your success. When you start thanking each person who has made a contribution to your life in some way, you will see the power of this simple, yet amazing part of etiquette.

Showing sincere appreciation to others is so important that I created a technique that I call the "Thank You Chain." For every workshop, keynote address, presentation, or referral I receive, I thank everyone who was involved in securing the opportunity. It is frequent that a project or business comes from a collective effort, and I want to make sure everyone knows that his or her part of it was deeply appreciated.

Start your own "Thank You Chain" by taking the following steps:

1. Working from past to present, think about the chain of events that led to your current career position or most recent business opportunity.

2. Make a list of the people who helped you through referrals, endorsements, advice, or in other ways.
3. Write, call, send a personalized e-mail, or my favorite—take out a pen and paper and write a handwritten note to thank them for their confidence in you. Report how you are doing and how their assistance positively impacted your success.
4. Each time you receive a new piece of business or advance in your career, keep them up to date and thank them again for the part they played.

One quality that makes people charismatic and positive networkers is their diligence in showing appreciation. I have heard it said that you can never say thank you too many times when it is done sincerely. It is good etiquette and good etiquette is always good business.

66/ Pulling It All Together

You might be getting overwhelmed with all the tips and ideas in this book. Just stop, choose one or two tips, and think how they might work in your life and work. Read the following as almost a summary-mantra any time you are ready to put this book away, no matter where you are.

You can meet people and network anyplace, anytime. Networking is a "nonstop" process; it is just living your life, connecting with people, and making things happen. Many people give up on networking because they think it is only about handing out business cards and asking for referrals. Nothing could be further from the truth. Building the relationships you need to reach your potential is easier than you think, yet it does take work. Look at it as a simple five-step process.

1. Meet people. Welcome opportunities to meet new people, and re-connect with those you already know.
2. Listen and learn. Everybody likes to talk about themselves. When you listen, you will learn who they are, what is important to them, how you can help them, and how they can help you.
3. Make connections. Help people connect with others you know who can help them.

4. Follow up. If you promise to do something, keep your promise, and do it in a timely manner.

5. Stay in touch to stay on the radar screen. After an initial period of contact, if nothing happens, most people will just move on. Here is where a networking system really "works" for successful networkers. Successful networkers find ways to stay in touch and continue to build relationships. Why? Because their goal is to build a network of long-lasting, mutually beneficial relationships, not just to get an immediate "result."

Recently, I read an article on loyalty written by someone at Unysis, a loyalty systems company. I noticed in his bio that he had gone to my alma mater, the University of Chicago, and contacted him. We met and this eventually let to my speaking engagement at their annual conference for executives working on frequent flyer programs in St. Paul de Venice. Great conference, great contacts.

—Steven Georgeou, Geocom, Inc.

67/ Do Your Research

Before you attend a meeting, research who is organizing it. Research the speakers, the topics, and the issues relevant to the meeting. The Internet can help you with much of your investigation. Much of the information you learn will lead to opportunities for you to start a conversation with others at the meeting. Be prepared with "get to know you" questions to ask individuals beyond information about the organization or event. These can be questions related to the work they do or to family, travel, hobbies, or favorite books or movies.

68/ Set A Goal For Every Event You Attend

Set a goal before you leave the office to meet two new people at any given event. This does not mean you cannot meet more than two. However, your goal is to meet just two new people with whom you will engage in conversation, ask some open-ended questions, and exchange pleasantries. If there is a reason to meet again, send a note, e-mail, or call to set up a follow-up meeting over breakfast or lunch. In any event, send a short "thank you for your time and conversation" to the two people even if there is no future meeting. This is just common courtesy and will serve you well as a respected leader.

The key is to set a goal to make a certain number of quality connections at every meeting, gathering, or event you attend. It is perfectly fine to seek out people you already know at an event. While meeting and connecting with new people is an important part of networking, staying in touch and nurturing relationships with those you already know is also very effective networking. And be sure to follow up.

The story starts at my friend's marriage in 1976. I was single and sitting at a table with Tom M. and his wife. We had a wonderful time exchanging stories and recollections of the "happy couple" and how we knew them. We did not see each other again until 1982. This is how it happened.

In 1978 I worked for Coopers & Lybrand in NY. In my capacity as a human resources manager I worked with the regional offices throughout the US, including the Boston Office. Jan was my contact and we spoke extensively, although had never met. When, in 1981, I left C&L and started in the executive search business, I told Jan that if she was ever in New York to please let me know and we would meet for a drink. She called me in 1982 to say that she was "dating" someone in NY and would love to meet for a drink. We met at Windows on the World and during the course of our conversation, she told me all about the new man in her life. The description sounded an awful lot like the Tom that I had met with his (first) wife at the wedding in 1976. It indeed turned out that this was the same person and on my way home that evening I stopped to say hello to him at One of By Land restaurant in the Village with Jan. I walked in and he remembered me instantly. We exchanged stories and despite the fact that Tom dated many more woman after Jan, we have established a very long friendship that has included sharing in each other's weddings, baptisms, promotions, divorces, graduations, and I'm sure the weddings of our children in the future. He really is a lifelong friend! We have shared so much happiness and sorrow with each other.

As I look back to why we reconnected, it was from our

first meeting at our friend's wedding where we shared sto-
ries about ourselves. There really was a connection from
the start. I have had many situations like this in my life. I
believe that there are people who come into our lives at cer-
tain times and then reappear when we are ready, but it is that
initial foundation that portends that future relationship.
—Eileen Finn, Eileen Finn & Associates

69/ Low Cost Networking Tips for Small Business Owners

As small business owners, we make major investments in marketing through Web sites, trade shows, and collateral materials. To augment these more expensive efforts, here are some low-cost, easy ways to stay in touch with clients. They work, and only take a short amount of time. Commit to several each week, and watch your business grow.

1. **Use the 41-cent investment plan.** The post office is alive and well—and even though the price of a stamp goes up, I believe it is worth it for the impression you make when you drop a note in the mail. Mail personal handwritten notes to your clients to say thank you for their business every time. It is a pleasant way to show your appreciation, and it keeps your name in front of them.

2. **Keep your eye on the news.** Go through the papers and magazines with a "marketing" eye. Send articles to clients or prospects that would be interesting to them. Attach a note saying, "Thought you might enjoy this." It shows people that you are thinking of them.

3. **Call with a tip.** When you have some relevant information or any thoughts or suggestions, call a few select clients and share the news. Even leaving a voice mail says to others, "I'm thinking of you and want to keep you informed." It also shows that you care about their businesses and want to help them grow.

4. **Seek advice.** Everyone likes to feel needed. When you call a client or prospect and say, "Help me out; I'd like your advice on something," you're giving that person a very high compliment, which will be remembered.

5. **Keep the door open.** Even when you lose an order or a bid, take the time to send sincere follow-up notes to let

clients know that you appreciate the time and consideration they gave you.

These tips take very little time and yet have a big pay-off. I have doubled my business for the last two years by using these tactics sincerely and consistently.

Networking is a life-long process. Every contact you meet offers you the chance to learn something new. These contacts enrich your life and lead you to relationships that help you achieve your goals.

chapter 5

Where to Network— EVERYWHERE!

Never Underestimate Your Hairdresser

Back in 2003, I had written a book for women in business to help promote the ideology behind the Downtown Women's Club, a local Boston organization at the time. I included a bit about how my hairdresser always helped me with networking by introducing me to his other clients, or keeping me in touch with some friends who he now saw more than I did. He loved being in the book and showed it to all his clients (and even sold some for me). One of his clients bought the book and gave it to her daughter. The daughter, Jessica, then e-mailed me to tell me how much she loved the book and wanted to know if she could start a Downtown Women's Club chapter in New York City. That call set off a great expansion and five years later I'm still working with Jessica who built the NYC chapter to nearly 2,000 members, and the DWC is in 10 cities and growing.

—Diane K. Danielson

70/ Places to Connect

To give you some "food for thought," here are some places I have made connections—see how you can add to it:

⊙ **The post office, at the back of the line**
   I was waiting in line at the post office when I struck up a conversation with the person in front of me. The conversation turned to my book which I just happened to be carrying. I always carry my books—they are my biggest business cards. If you have one or some other "prop," carry it with you at all times. It turned out my fellow post office customer worked with a small manufacturing company that was looking for a consultant to do almost exactly

my services. We exchanged cards, I followed up, and we are building the rapport and relationship.

- ⊙ **The post office, at the front of the line**
  As I reached the front of the line, I began talking with the clerk, to whom I had previously given a copy of my book. While we talked, I found out the man liked the book so much he was going to recommend to upper management that copies of the book be bought for post offices throughout New York! I wish I could say that it has happened. However it is taking a lot of time—it is the government, after all!

- ⊙ **The nail salon**
  I was having my nails done one day when I heard another customer chatting about holiday plans. Starting a conversation while our nails dried, I found out the woman was looking for speakers to talk to members of her company as part of their training. I left the salon with freshly polished nails and two business leads.

- ⊙ **The coffee shop**
  I was sitting in a coffee shop talking with a friend about his advertising business. Noticing that a man at the next table was listening, I introduced myself and asked if he was in advertising as well. He said he was but was currently looking for a job. I introduced the two men and later heard that the man at the next table had been granted an interview at my friend's business.

These common themes are why I say, "You never know," and many of the people you meet in everyday life could be a potential networking contact. I have also gathered solid business contacts:

- ⊙ On an airplane.
- ⊙ At the dentist's office
- ⊙ In line for movie tickets
- ⊙ Having a dress altered.

The point is to be constantly aware of opportunities to meet new people, because you never know who will turn out to be a great networking contact. As I've said before, always be prepared with your conversation starter. Don't ask for something; offer something. Follow up.

Good networking consists of practicing good communication skills on a consistent basis and being ready to use those skills in any situation, not just at conventions or when you're unemployed. The most important thing is to follow up, otherwise a casual conversation will never lead to a business relationship.

Dear Ms Andrea,

When you spoke at Washington U for our MBA you very kindly gifted my mother a copy of your book—at almost 50 she is starting her new Permanent Cosmetics business and your book has really helped her self-confidence. She just sent me an e-mail, and I thought I would share this snippet with you:

I am really enjoying Andrea Nierenberg's book. I have been trying the "People You Meet By Chance" networking angle. I take every opportunity to use this and it is fun for me to begin to talk to people in this way.

I went to pick up my license plate at the courthouse and the lady who waited on me needed eyebrows in a really bad way. I asked her if she could make out what my nametag says: ITA2EYZ. I told her I do Permanent Cosmetics. She said, "I have always wanted eyebrows." I gave her my card and she said she would definitely be calling me. We talked for awhile about what was involved with this procedure.

I do this every chance I get. Reading the book just makes it easier for me to try these things. Thank You!!

Thank you very much for making such a difference,
—Ryan Richt, MBA student, Washington University

71/ Practice Your Networking Skills

"Experience is a hard teacher because she gives the test first, the lesson afterwards."
—Vincent Sanders Law

Often we learn this lesson after we've been putting our networking strategy to work consistently. Answer the following questions today, next week, and in three months to analyze your "formal" networking progress as you go along:

- ⊙ What are my personal goals and objectives specific to networking?
- ⊙ What are some of the "rocks" that keep me from breaking that barrier?
- ⊙ How could I be more effective networking with my existing clients and how will I do this?
- ⊙ How do I effectively "work the room" at an event whether I am introverted or extroverted?
- ⊙ How do I make a memorable impact when meeting someone?
- ⊙ How do I strengthen my 20-second "sound bite?"
- ⊙ How do I effectively follow up?

72/ Join the Organizations Best for You and Use the 2-2-2 Strategy

If you have been in your business for a while, you probably know about all the various networking groups available. The question is, how do you choose which one will work for you? Choosing what group you join will determine the effectiveness of your time and money. I recommend a 2-2-2 strategy to decide which organizations and clubs to join. Before you decide to join a group, take these important steps.

1. **Attend two meetings.** This will help you in several ways:
   - ⊙ You will experience the organization or group first hand.
   - ⊙ You will see whether the organization will meet your particular needs.
   - ⊙ You will meet people involved in the organization.
   - ⊙ You can access a schedule of events and find out their long-term goals.
2. **Meet two people and exchange business cards.** This is an important step in understanding the organization for several reasons:
   - ⊙ You can ask specific questions about the organization, such as who regularly attends, if the meetings you attended are typical, and how you can benefit from the group.

- ⊙ These two contacts can introduce you to other members.
- ⊙ You can find out what kinds of people participate in the group.

3. **Arrange two follow-up meetings for breakfast, lunch, or coffee.** This step is great for its long-term benefits:
   - ⊙ If you join, these two relationships can multiply into many relationships within the group.
   - ⊙ Regardless of whether you join or not, you now have two new contacts!

By following this easy 2-2-2 Plan, you will find the organizations that best meet your needs. Join and become active in these organizations. If you choose your organizations carefully, you can use them to make important contacts, grow your business, and expand your network.

73/ Business Cards––for Travel Safety

My friend Joyce Newman, another busy road warrior, shared this tip with me. Place your business card in your coat pocket and a stash of them in your luggage and briefcase.

Just in case, you lose your luggage, someone could find you easily.

74/ "The Opposite of Networking Is Not Working"

Write this quote down and put in on your computer monitor. Every time you meet someone you have the opportunity to learn from them or to be a resource to them. It is all about giving first before getting anything back. This is my truest mantra. Look at it each morning and start the day with a goal for putting it into practice.

Here is an example. I got a call one morning from Eric with whom I had worked several years before—he was a participant in a workshop. He remembered me and had now moved to a new position. Turns out he was also looking for a new apartment and I had just spoken to a friend in the business who was describing a place that almost seemed perfect for him. I connected the two. Several months later he moved though not to the first apartment but to another my contact showed him. He then introduced her to three other friends who have all become her clients. I was thrilled— all because I think with that "headset" on.

You might say—did it come back? Remember not to keep score—because things do come back down the road. Eric did in fact have me work with his new company and then introduced me to two other friends and I have now worked for them also.

So, yes, your network will expand and grow, just as you want it to—however you must give and be willing to give and let the relationship grow first.

75/ Start a Conversation Today

Approach someone and do not wait for them to approach you. The key to creating connections is conversation. The secret of conversation is to ask open-ended high-gain questions, like "What kind of work do you do?" "What brought you to this event?" The quality of the information you receive depends on the quality of your questions. When you have a conversation, it may lead to a business relationship. A relationship could lead to new business. A business relationship when nurtured can and will lead to long-term continued success.

You have to meet someone new in order to welcome and create these opportunities. If nothing else, you will hone your presentation skills and that is always a major plus.

> ### The Plain Truth about Networking
> One of the golden rules of business has long been: "It isn't what you know, but who you know."
>
> While this little piece of advice has significant implications for all of us, it begs the more important question: "Who don't I know, and what and who do they know that I should know?" Of course, the logical follow up is "Where and how do I get to know them?"
>
> As my good friend Andrea will tell you, you can't leave your home or office with the intent that you are going to run into someone and create a network opportunity. Staring at name tags is more likely to create a sore neck than it is an important business or social connection. That said, one should also be prepared to network when an unexpected opportunity arises. Know your own elevator speech. Always try to smile and always be aware of what is going on around you.

One of my most successful connections occurred under the most unusual circumstances, and it is worth sharing because we turned an innocent question into an important opportunity and eventually into a long term relationship.

Back in 1980—long before I even knew what networking was—one of my great passions in life was collecting rare old baseball cards. Back then, baseball card collecting was still an under-the-radar hobby and it was difficult to communicate with other collectors except at shows—and most of those were limited to one's local area. For me personally, there was a great deal to learn and very few people to learn from. One of the most knowledgeable people in the world was a British collector named Sir Edward Wharton Tigar.

As fate would have it, I was doing some research in the Print Room of the Metropolitan Museum of Art and looking at some rare cards. Unexpectedly, someone asked to borrow some yellow paper and my pencil. The accent was distinguished and unmistakably British. As I turned to my new colleague I stated: "You have a English accent; by chance do you know that distinguished British card collector, Sir Edward Wharton Tigar?"

To my astonishment he replied, "It is I." And thus began a seven year friendship (until his passing). A wonderful interchange of knowledge, a few card trades, and some lovely social evenings. As it turns out Sir Edward was a world class thinker and one of the most interesting people I ever met (certainly the most interesting I ever met by accident).

—Bruce Dorskind, The Dorskind Group

76/ Re-connect with Contacts You Already Know

Find ways to nurture relationships. Here are a few hints. I know I'm repeating myself, yet these are vital to your success:

- ⊙ **Listen and learn**. Everyone likes to talk about themselves. When you listen, you will learn who they are, what is important to them, how you can help them, and how they can help you.
- ⊙ **Make connections**. Help people connect with others you know who can help them.

- ⊙ **Follow up**. When you promise to do something, keep your promise and do it in a timely fashion.
- ⊙ **Stay in touch**. After an initial period of follow-ups, even if no business has resulted from those initial contacts find ways to stay in touch. This way you'll continue to build a network of longlasting, mutually beneficial relationships.

77/ Keep Contacts on Your Radar

At work . . . at the health club or other personal activities . . . at the store . . . on a trip . . . in your community—keep people on your radar. I buy client and friend gifts when I see something they would like (refer back to my contact information list at the beginning of chapter 4). One of my clients loves giraffes. Knowing this, I've been able to find the most unusual "giraffe gifts" for her. It is on my radar about her and I seem to find things everywhere. Think about your own clients and friends. It is like "red cars." You may never see them or "notice them," until you decide to buy one and then they seem to be EVERYWHERE!

78/ Do It NOW—Every Day Instead of Only Waiting for Holidays

Every day is a holiday when you remember someone. When I was in a Los Angeles hotel gift shop, I found a book of New York poems for my friend Bruce (I know, NY poems in LA?!), as well as two leather notebooks for friends, one who is writing his life stories and one who loves to keep a journal . I also found an unusual candle for anther client who uses them to decorate her office. Alert yourself and think as you find something along your daily path: Who might like and enjoy this?

79/ The Business "Setting" or Elevator Awareness

Always be ready and able to pull out the answers to the following questions whenever you meet a new contact:

- ⊙ At a trade show, meeting, convention, or a client call— what is your business pitch?
- ⊙ Do you have your networking tool kits at all times—ready to hand out business cards and/or record "information" about new contacts or update previous contacts?

Remember, Do the Big Step—approach someone new Get out of your comfort zone. Networking is a leadership skill you'll develop as you practice your communication skills. Be the leader—form your own group; participate in your local professional organization's board; get involved with your community; mentor others as they move up in their careers; teach others in organizational courses or workshops; volunteer to make a speech on a subject pertinent to your group; write and publish articles; create your own Web site as a marketing tool.

Recognize that good relationships require nurturing, not "work," and genuine results cannot be forced when you meet new people. They develop over time as you get to know and appreciate each other.

80/ Networking Takes Time and Patience

When we network, we must learn to respect others' timetables. Of course, sometimes new contacts do not respond in a timely fashion. They may be busy with their own deadlines and have a lot of responsibilities, and therefore cannot immediately respond to you. So how can we move the networking process forward without "pushing" too hard?

Ask your contact how he or she wants to be contacted. Some people prefer that everything be done in writing, while others would rather receive a quick follow-up phone call or e-mail alerting them to new opportunities that can benefit them.

Check on new contacts regularly. Often in sales, the advice is to deal quickly with people—without having a long-term follow-up plan in place. In my experience the long-term follow up is often much more important. Mark your calendar for the next significant date on your contacts' calendar. For instance, you can phone or e-mail them a month before new bids are sent out, or even mention that you hope to connect with them at an upcoming trade show.

Develop a networking game plan. New contacts will not develop into anything important without long term nurturing. Keep a list of all contacts readily available. Using that list, develop a plan that is appropriate for each of your contacts. Some may be reached through one general method, like a newsletter, others will require unique treatment. For instance, an effective follow up for some contacts may be as simple as seeking them out at an upcoming business function, while another contact might appreciate a note with helpful information on a subject you've discussed previously.

Once you discover what is effective, build on what works and develop the skills you need, such as writing and speaking to make meaningful connections with those important people.

81/ Making Networking Practical

There are two main areas of focus when using positive networking tactics: how contacts are identified and appropriate follow-up.

Identifying Potential Contacts

Once you understand how to approach networking from a positive standpoint, you can use techniques that are specific for each of the following categories of contacts:

- ⊙ **Satisfied customers.** What better referral? They can be the best advocates because they know what you have to offer. You can ask them to introduce you to other people. Most importantly, thank them with a personal note or phone call.
- ⊙ **Friends.** We work hard at building our friendships, including mutual trust. You can find out about your friends' work and help them. Then when the time is right, you can ask them for a referral.
- ⊙ **Neighbors.** Make the effort to strike up conversations with people in your building or neighborhood. You'll often find out that you have common interests with them.
- ⊙ **Happy, helpful people.** These are the people all of us meet by chance or connect with in unexpected ways. You might meet them on a plane, train, or waiting in line at the movies. Life has a funny way of connecting us when we least expect it. We just have to be ready for the opportunity.

Follow-up Tactics

Effective networking is based on simple tactics. Here are my Seven Rules of Networking to live by:

1. **Smile**. A smile is a universal welcome sign. The people we meet for the first time will appreciate our warmth.

2. **Look the person in the eye**. It's a compliment to look at someone. It's a way to connect with someone new in the shortest time possible.

3. **Listen**. One of the greatest compliments we can give other people is to let them know that we are listening to them. Remember, when we are networking with new contacts, it's like reading the paper. Let people tell their stories so we can discover the "news we can use."

4. **Pay attention to body language**. First impressions are lasting ones. Monitor expressions. Sometimes, we need to loosen up because meeting new people can make us tense.

5. **Avoid being pushy**. Avoid coming on too strong. Even if you just lost your job, don't let anyone think that you are desperate.

6. **Give genuine compliments**. Yes, even with new contacts, a compliment might be appropriate. When we listen to people carefully, often they will mention something that they are proud of. We need to think for a moment and find a way to sincerely acknowledge others' achievements.

7. **Business cards are golden**. Ask for people's cards, yet only offer yours when requested. When we do get their cards, we should treat them as fine treasures and give them the most respect.

Networking is a process, one that can create business connections to last a lifetime. As someone who works in sales, you are constantly developing, building, and cultivating relationships that can give you results beyond your expectations.

82/ Power of Three Personal Communications in Networking

"The power of three" consists of writing a follow-up note to three contacts a day. The United States Postal Service tells us that only 4 percent of the mail is personalized. Therefore, sending notes will put your company ahead of 96 percent of the competition. Here are some good examples where personal notes work particularly well:

⊙ "Heard something good about you." If you hear about someone's personal achievement or if you read something

positive about their company, that provides a good opportunity to send a note.

⊙ "Give away information." For example, if you participate in
a Chamber of Commerce, invite a contact to join you as
your guest for a special program by sending a note with a
copy of the event.

⊙ "Gone, yet not forgotten." Even if your contacts have clearly
stated that they are not interested right now in communicating with you, a follow-up note offering some valuable
information is a good way to keep current and potential
customers aware of your company.

83/ Developing Your 20-Second Infomercial

In chapter 2 we discussed your PBS, or Personal Brand Statement, and why it is important when you meet new people, to let
them know quickly and clearly who you are and what you are.
You need to do this in a way that is concise, enthusiastic, and
memorable. Sometimes a PBS is too long. You may only have time
for a 20-second "infomercial" about yourself that keeps people
interested using the following S.T.R.A.T.E.G.Y:

S   Make your infomercial Short and Succinct.
T   Think of it in advance.
R   Remember the Results you want to achieve.
A   Be Articulate in your message.
T   Time is of the essence—20 seconds or less is optimal.
E   Speak with Enthusiasm and Energy.
G   Set a Goal to attain.
Y   Focus on the "You" (the other person).

If you carefully plan how you introduce yourself, you will start
dynamic conversations that will lead to more information about
your new contact and ways you can keep meeting. Always make
the person you are speaking with curious and interested. Tell them
something that will stay in their mind when they think of you. The
bottom line is to introduce yourself in a way that will make people
want to know you better. Developing those relationships is the
heart of networking.

chapter 6

Networking Etiquette

Etiquette is no more than showing respect for other people's feelings and sensitivities, and learning to be an effective networker involves the same kind of respect for the people you meet. It takes networking etiquette to turn chance acquaintances into long term friends and business associates. It's about building trust; displaying respect, good manners, and common courtesy are key.

84/ The Ten Rules of Business Etiquette

Here are my rules of business etiquette that will make networking at events and meetings a positive experience:

1. **It's better to arrive early than late.** An early arrival shows enthusiasm for the event and respect for other people's time. It also affords you the opportunity to meet more people. As my friend Gil Robinov says, "If you are on time, you are late."

2. **Position your name tag so people can easily see it.** Place your name tag on your right hand lapel. When meeting contacts, this will allow people to see your name better as they shake your right hand.

3. **Exchange business cards with ease and grace.** Plenty of fresh, neat business cards are a must. Place them in a pocket where they are easily accessible and be sure to keep yours separate from the cards you receive.

4. **Silently communicate your interest.** Make eye contact and keep it. It is noticeable when your eyes are wandering around the room searching for a "better" contact. Looking someone in the eye shows respect and interest.

5. **Extend a confident greeting.** Make your handshake firm, professional, and genuine. Bone crusher or jellyfish

handshakes come across as intimidating or insecure. A sincere greeting will make a lasting impression.

6. **Avoid invading personal space**. Be aware of your contact's personal space. Moving in too close while conversing makes people uncomfortable. Most people consider anything closer than 18 inches too close and will back away from you.

7. **Gracefully join conversations.** Be sure to ask for permission to join a conversation in progress. Simply say, "This looks like a fun group, may I join in?" or "How do you all know each other?" You can tailor your request to fit your personality. People enjoy having you connect with them when you are courteous.

8. **Avoid the awkwardness of food to chew and handle while you converse.** While many events and meetings offer refreshments, try not to be eating and carrying on a conversation at the same time. It takes a lot of experience to balance a plate and eat while conversing. I don't recommend it.

9. **Nonalcoholic networking is the best.** A nonalcoholic drink without ice is the easiest to handle. Why no ice? Frigid handshakes are unpleasant. Why nonalcoholic? You'll pay better attention.

10. **Politely exit conversations.** Your objective at networking events should be to develop several connections. Talking with someone, learning about them and how to follow up, exchanging business cards, and moving on is an accepted practice. When exiting a conversation, politely express pleasure at having met the individual and the hope that you will meet again. Develop your strategy and follow-up.

Successful business relationships, just like successful personal relationships, rely on common courtesy. Following these simple rules of etiquette will create a more relaxing opportunity for networking and your ability to be well-received at events or meetings.

85/ How to Exit with Grace

Networking events are full of professionals to whom you can be of service or who can help you. In these situations, be sure to consider other people's time, as they may also have others to meet during an event. Set your own goals to meet people, but learn to exit gracefully when you've finished your conversation. Here are some polite exit lines that allow you to leave without offense:

- ⊙ "It was great meeting you, and I hope we can continue our conversation sometime over lunch or coffee."
- ⊙ "Thanks for sharing the information about your new project. It sounds exciting. Best of continued success."
- ⊙ "Please excuse me, I see a friend I'd like to go over and visit with. Enjoy your evening."
- ⊙ "Let me introduce you to (name of another nearby colleague). He may be a good person to discuss some of the opportunities you have."
- ⊙ "I'm so glad we met. Lots of good luck, and if I hear of anything that might be a fit for you, I'll definitely be in touch."
- ⊙ "I enjoyed hearing about your company and look forward to seeing you again."

Before starting your exit, always ask for a business card. Remember to follow up with at least a short note and perhaps a phone call to arrange a future meeting. Over time, you'll begin to build rapport and learn about each other, as you establish a solid business relationship. Also at events, realize that people want to talk with others, so never monopolize anyone for too long—I advise only seven to ten minutes.

86/ A Simple Note Goes a Long Way

After any meeting, it is important to connect with your new contacts and follow up with your friends or acquaintances to nurture them. Because timing is of the essence, be sure to follow up quickly, efficiently, and genuinely. It is the key to growing your network and business by building your contacts, connections, and trusted advisors. The following are the four "Must-Dos" after a meeting:

1. **Generate a greeting.** Within twenty-four hours after a meeting, send a note, e-mail, or place a call to let your new contacts know how much you appreciated getting to know them. Doing this distinguishes you and makes you stand out.
2. **Present your promise.** When you promised to send materials, call to set up a meeting, or give a referral, keep your word. Following up with the materials you promised

in a timely manner will establish you as a trustworthy person. As I've said before: Under-promise and over-deliver.

3. **Dial the digits.** Within two weeks after suggesting a get-together, call your new contact and set up lunch or a more formal meeting. Always send a courtesy e-mail or call to confirm the day before. Your sincerity and professionalism will shine through.

4. **Give the gift of thanks.** When a contact provides you with a referral or offers to pass your information along, be sure to say thank you and keep him or her in the loop by letting them know the developments and results that occur. These simple gestures of appreciation go a long way when building your network.

    Thanking contacts for their time and their attention is an important way to show them your respect. Offering them something tangible like a referral, information, or a simple meal shows you care. Remember, people do business with those whom they know, respect, and often like.

87/ The Power of the Personal Note

I feel so strongly about the power of the personal note, I want to emphasize it further in this tip. The art of writing personal notes is sadly disappearing. A personal note is one of the best ways to connect and re-connect with others. Just as a reminder, here are seven reasons to send a thank you note:

- ⊙ For time and consideration
- ⊙ For a compliment you received
- ⊙ For a piece of advice given
- ⊙ For business
- ⊙ For a referral
- ⊙ For a gift
- ⊙ For help on a project

Thank You Notes

Thank you notes are one of the least expensive and most effective networking tools. Always carry notes and stamps with you. Then, whenever you have some "found time"—in an airport, on a train, waiting at a doctor's office, or watching TV—you can dash off a note, address it, and pop it in the mail.

FYI Notes

Don't forget those "FYI notes" that show you have your contact's best interests in mind and help you keep in touch at any time. You can send many things, such as clippings or articles, to a person. This lets them know several things:

⊙ You were thinking of them when you read it
⊙ You know what they are interested in
⊙ You care about their business

Notes of Congratulations

Congratulations are a perfect opportunity to let someone know you are cheering them on. You can give these out on many occasions:

⊙ Promotions
⊙ An award or honor
⊙ An anniversary

Nice Talking to (or Meeting) You Notes

These thoughtful notes help a person to remember you fondly. You can send these out after several events:

⊙ A meeting
⊙ A chance encounter
⊙ A phone conversation

88/ The Power of E-mail

E-mail is not quite as personal as a handwritten note, yet it is a powerful way to keep in touch with your network regularly and our most efficient form of business communication. Here are a few guiding principles for making your e-mails count:

⊙ Keep your e-mails brief and focused.
⊙ Use meaningful subject lines.
⊙ Use a format: purpose, body, and action.
⊙ If you need to send a long document, send it as an attachment.
⊙ Do not forward jokes, chain letters, warnings about viruses, or other junk mail that is making its rounds throughout

the Internet. It is unprofessional and a waste of everyone's time.

⊙ Always re-read your message before you hit send. Make sure your tone is what you want it to be. Avoid anything that could be construed as sarcasm or innuendo.

⊙ Answer all e-mails within 24 hours. If you are going to be away from your computer, use the "away from my desk until . . ." message available in most e-mail programs.

When my office administrator was new, she was working with the e-mail system and sent out a test with some comment (not offensive at all, just some test words). Well, it went to all our patients who had e-mail . . . So, never put anything in an e-mail you do not want repeated.
                              —Allan M. Miller, DDS, FAGD

89/ Who Introduces Whom

In today's business world, making proper introductions is often essential to finding new contacts. Whether in person, through e-mail, or over the phone, polite professional conduct is essential to keeping and and growing your network. Here are Nierenberg's Rules of Order:

1. Defer to position and age. Gender is not a factor. An introduction is normally made in the following order—the younger less senior executive or person TO the older:

    ⊙ Introduce younger to older
    ⊙ Introduce your company peer to a peer in another company
    ⊙ Introduce a junior to a senior executive
    ⊙ Introduce a fellow executive to a client
    ⊙ Introduce a personal contact to a business contact.

2. When making introductions, give a brief statement about each person's interest or profession, or better yet, something the two might have in common. This is polite and gets the conversation going.

3. Avoid using nicknames unless it is the person's business name. Use full names and titles such as "Dr." to

show respect when you know they always use it.

4. Speak slowly and clearly so each name can be heard.

90/ Good Manners at Non-networking Events

Nonstop networkers find places and times to network outside of scheduled meetings and business events. Whether in an elevator, at a sporting event, or waiting in line, we are always looking for ways to connect with others. We networkers are eager to meet people who may become our friends and business associates, any place any time

However, we also know that networking inappropriately can be destructive to possible relationships. It is important to be considerate both of the person to whom we are talking and to those around us. Here are a few ways to avoid embarrassment for yourself and your potential contact.

⊙ Recognize where you are and what you are there for. For example, at a funeral, respect and consideration for the bereaved are far more important than meeting acquaintances.

⊙ Be prepared to graciously suggest that you talk about business at a more appropriate time and place. You could say, "Perhaps this is not a good time to discuss business, may I give you a call on (date) and we could discuss this further, (consider some options), (I could help you out)?"

⊙ Ask permission before exchanging business cards, and do so discreetly.

⊙ Remember that some establishments, such as private clubs, simply do not allow the conducting of business. Be aware of this and follow the prescribed behavior.

Successful networkers care about the person they are speaking with as well as those around them. Showing respect is one of the best ways to make and keep contacts. Network whenever and wherever you can, just do so with discretion, so that you will avoid embarrassment or giving offense.

During the summer of 2000, after my sophomore year at Rice University, I became an intern for Enercorp, a renewable energy company in Morocco. Upon my return to the US that August, I was waiting for my friend to pick me up at

JFK airport and noticed a gentleman standing next to me who had been on my flight. Eventually he asked me if I had flown from London to New York on business. I told him that I'd been a summer intern in Morocco, and we got to talking about Moroccan politics. He was kind enough to introduce himself as the General Counsel of the Americas for Unilever. He gave me his card, said he had to run, but asked me to call him so we could chat.

The next day I called him, and within five minutes he called me back and asked if I could meet him the next day at 4:30. I was two days from leaving for France to study abroad for my junior year and I was supposed to leave for Washington DC that same night to see my brother (whom I had not seen in a long while). Apologetically I told him that I was supposed to leave for Washington. His exact response was, "Well, that's a shame, I would have really liked to speak with you." I was shocked that someone at such a high level was so generous and seemed genuine. I decided in a split second that I was going to cancel my trip to Washington, and meet the gentleman the next day at 4:30. Upon meeting him, he told me, "Of the many people I have asked to come meet me, you are one of two people who have taken advantage of it, and you're the only one who took advantage of it the next day. That initiative is what makes people successful."

Since that day, Ron and I have remained close, and he has been a true mentor to me, as I have run by him every large decision I've had to make since that day seven years ago. His commitment to being my mentor is impeccable, as he has guided me through my professional and educational decisions. Whether he is closing a huge deal in New York, or working with senior management abroad, he always calls me to discuss my thoughts. My appreciation for him cannot be expressed.

This example, to me, shows the true value of taking the initiative to reach out to someone, even if you have only spoken briefly to them. You never know what can happen!

—Prakash Venkataraman,
Sponsors for Educational Opportunity

91/ Shy Polite People, You Can Network Too

I have a confession to make. You are an introvert. That's fine, SO AM I, and in many ways we have an advantage over our more assertive colleagues.

You may feel that despite all your knowledge of networking, you are too shy to network successfully. The idea that networking is only for people with outgoing personalities is really false. Introverts have strengths that they can use with strategies that blend well with their personalities. Here are some real advantages that introverts have for networking:

- ⊙ Introverts are usually great listeners. They would rather let another person do the talking, and that shows respect toward their colleague.
- ⊙ They remember details about their contacts, which others might miss. Since they are listening, they can take in more information about their contact.
- ⊙ They focus on the person they are talking to, making that person feel significant.
- ⊙ They build sound relationships and care for them because they are often helpful individuals who watch out for others.
- ⊙ They find the right time to speak—never interrupting or asserting their opinions.
- ⊙ They are helpful, which often makes others want to be helpful in return.
- ⊙ They network very well in situations where they can use their skill to help others.

I've found that introverts are almost always passionate about a certain aspect of their business, industry, or product. They speak naturally with enthusiasm and conviction about the things that matter to them. Often, they've learned to overcome their shyness by discussing something they are passionate about. They become extremely effective when they have focus and a genuine reason to make a contact.

By building upon your strengths, Introverts, you will become effective networkers. Because you already listen well, help others when you can, and speak well when you are passionate about something, you have the skills to build and nurture strong relationships, which are the keys to great networking.

92/ The Courtesy and Cultivation of Listening Skills

Listening politely shows respect, and is an essential part of making a real connection with people. If you don't listen carefully to what people have to tell you, how can you help them and learn how they can help you?

Rate yourself on a scale of 1 to 5 on these essential active listening skills. Give yourself a 5 if, "I always do this with ease and confidence," and 1 if, "I rarely do this and feel awkward when I do."

1. I make eye contact. I always look the other person in the eye during our conversation and focus my full attention on him or her. If it's difficult to me to continue eye contact, I look at the person's "third eye," a spot just above the bridge of the nose between the eyes, realizing that we can only look at one eye at a time anyway.

2. I ask questions for clarification. If I don't understand, I ask the other person to explain so that I can understand better.

3. I show concern by acknowledging feelings. I also listen with my eyes. I use positive body language by nodding and smiling when appropriate.

4. I try to understand the speaker's point of view before giving mine. I recognize that the other person is far more interested in stating his or her point of view than in hearing mine.

5. I am poised and emotionally controlled. I refrain from jumping to conclusions or interrupting with what I want to say when the other person is speaking.

6. I react nonverbally with a smile or a nod. I know this shows my interest and allows the person to continue without interruption.

7. I pay close attention and do not let my mind wander. I am careful not to allow my mind to take a mental excursion.

8. I avoid interrupting. I always let the other person finish.

9. I avoid changing the subject without warning. Changing the subject abruptly relays that you are not listening and only want to talk about whatever is on your mind.

How did you do?

If you scored 35-45, you're an **exceptional listener!**

If you scored 25-34, you're a **very good listener.**

If you scored 20-24, you're an **average listener.**

If you scored 15-19, keep working, you'll improve . . . and maybe get those Q-Tips out!

Take a good look at the areas where your rating could improve. Start to work on these, while continuing to practice the skills you've already mastered. Take the test again in two weeks. Watch how your ratings increase when you commit to improving your listening skills!

Little Things Make Big Differences

While publisher of a national trade magazine, I received a call one morning from a consultant who was doing some research on a topic that I was fairly familiar with.

As is my standard practice, I provided her with as much information as I could and then named some additional resources. The whole process took approximately 20 minutes. Fast forward one year later. My sales team was having a difficult time getting an appointment with the new president of a company that represented some strong opportunities.

They asked me to personally call the president's assistant to schedule the meeting using my "publisher title."With no resistance the meeting was set for the following week. Assuming that my sales team was correct and that the president was more interested in seeing the publisher than the sales team, off we went to the meeting.

Immediately following our introductions, the president, whose first name is Diane, turned to me and said, "Do you remember me?" No, I shyly replied wondering what she was referring to. She then recounted the story of how helpful I'd been in providing her with data a year earlier.

"Now do you remember?" I still couldn't, explaining that helping people with business information is just something I enjoy doing, and thus do it on a weekly basis and don't usually recall names.

So Diane explained that when she was a consultant, I was the only one to take her call and assist her; yet now that she was president of a large company, everybody was happy to return her call. Without boring you with the rest of the details, our publication was one of the few given the time to present and was awarded the majority of their business for the next two years.

—Jeff Reinhardt, Berkery, Noyes & Co.

93/ Networking through Thoughtful Creativity, Persistence, and Respect

Previously we've discussed the importance of personal notes and personal time for nurturing contacts and developing stronger relationships. It's quite easy to write notes, but not so easy to create face-to-face time with people.

Remember my F.A.C.E. Tips?

F   Make it Fun and Friendly. Find unique things to do and places to meet.
A   Adapt to each other's timetable and surroundings.
C   Connect and find Common interests.
E   Know when to Exit. Be respectful of other people's time.

Here are some creative, pleasant ways to meet with your contacts in a cordial sociable way. Extend an invitation to:

- Meet for coffee, tea, or cappuccino—instead of the traditional breakfast, lunch, or dinner.
- Play a fun game of golf, tennis, or bridge.
- Go for an invigorating walk, spa treatment, or health club exercise date.
- Meet at a museum, art gallery, or store.
- Attend an industry event, cocktail party, or trade show.
- Join up for a play, concert, or sporting event.
- Share a cab to a meeting or meet at the sky club at the airport.

Be creative. Everyone is busy and business-focused and appreciates new and unique suggestions to relax and learn more about a thoughtful colleague.

94/ Persistence Pays Off—Be Patient

When I was selling advertising years ago, one of my contacts

suggested I get in touch with Bob Drucker, who was then responsible for the advertising at a major printing company. I wrote notes,
cards, called; nothing seemed to work, even with the introduction
from a mutual friend.

I decided to keep up the "campaign" and did not give up. Finally,
after about twenty cards, numerous calls, and even an anniversary card, he agreed to meet me for coffee at a trade show. Fifteen
years and several jobs later, Bob is still one of my good business
friends and clients.

Never give up when you know there might be some potential.

95/ Networking Is Not Bad Manners

1. **Give yourself permission to network.** Networking is as
   much about nurturing as it is going out to meet people.
   Changing your attitude to a positive one is the first step to
   networking success. Realize that "networking" is a state of
   mind and that it is pure people skills, courtesy, and developing connections. As you leave for work every day, give
   yourself a mental pep talk about connecting and reconnecting with people and setting a goal for yourself each
   week. Doing such simple things as, "I said hello to someone I didn't know well," or "I sent an e-mail to a colleague
   in another department" can be the first steps to networking success in your business.

2. **Prepare yourself by making a list of "opening lines"**
   to use when meeting someone new. Use open-ended questions that require more than a one-word answer, or at least
   follow up with an open-ended question like, "What brings
   you to this event?" or, "What industry or side of the business are you in?" Practice some opening lines with friends
   and colleagues so you will be prepared when you go to
   events. Engage the other person by moving attention from
   yourself to the other person. Niceness is still key. A warm
   and approachable smile is always a great icebreaker and
   the start to your opening lines.

3. **Have your 20-second infomercial about yourself ready**
   and practice it until it becomes spontaneous and natural.
   Ask yourself, "How do I want to be remembered? What is
   the headline that will grab someone and what is the actual
   benefit statement when I say what I do?" It is not about a

title—such as "I'm the vice president of (fill in the blank—it is all the same!)." More important is *what* do you do, so that someone says: "Tell me more." Tell your story well to avoid what I call the "so what" factor.

4. **Use the Internet** to establish some relationships with those in your field—specifically for the introverted style. Online acquaintances can become an important part of your network. Plan to meet them at professional conferences and trade shows.

5. **Do your research before attending an event.** Learn the basics about the organization and the people likely to be there. This kind of preliminary research will give you the knowledge you need to focus your conversation on the goals and accomplishments of the people you meet and earn their interest in you. Here is a quick checklist of questions to answer before you go:

   - Who is being honored or speaking?
   - Who will be there—any chance of getting an advance copy of attendees?
   - Who do you already know who will be there?
   - What can you learn about them in advance?

6. **Set a goal for yourself to meet and connect** with at least three people, and develop your list of "get to know you" questions to help you meet this goal. These should go deeper than "opening line" questions; and, as I've said, help you to get to know the interests of the people you meet. Rapport develops as you start asking and gently probing, never "grilling or drilling," and respond to what you learn about the other person and perhaps relate those interests to what you do and how you do it.

96/ Polite Get-to-Know-You Questions

These are examples of the kinds of open-ended, cordial questions that invite contacts to converse with you:

- If you could do any kind of work, what would it be, and what makes you say that?
- What do you do when you're not at work—family, hobbies

or special interests?
- How did you get involved in this industry or group?
- What books or movies or plays have you seen recently?
- What do you like the most about your work and why?
- When you work with ___ (lawyers, bankers, consultants, etc.), what do you look for that makes your job and life easier?

97/ Nurturing, More Long-Range Questions

These are my all time favorites, which give me a reason to follow up and stay in touch—whether it will be on the short term or long range goal:

- How do I know when I'm either speaking to a potential client or job opportunity or person you would like to meet?
- What is your preferred method of communication for staying in touch?

It is only after I have asked, listened to, and understood their responses these questions that I can bring the conversation back to something about me. For example, when someone says, "We're looking for consultants who really customize their work to our company and stay on the project from beginning to end," I might say, "I totally agree with you, because when I recently worked with XYZ company, the leading reason I got the project was for customization, delivery, and follow through." Then I offer a short example of each.

The whole goal is getting people to open up so that they are talking about a subject near and dear to them, and we can develop cooperation and rapport. It is only by understanding people's needs that we can demonstrate sincere interest by basing our responses on them.

98/ To Keep the Conversation Going—Keep a Journal of "Small Talk" Topics

Inform yourself about what is happening in the world, and keep a journal of such things as current events, industry topics, books and movies, community topics, sports, celebrities, other items that engage people in the world around us. Start your notebook and let it grow.

Here's another hint, if the conversation has strayed from topics you feel comfortable discussing or topics you want to return to, use a "bridge" phrase such as, "That reminds me of . . ." and link it get back to the topic you had started.

99/ Sincere Compliments

Make a goal to look for positive attributes in the people you meet and give five compliments a day. When you look for them, you will find them—then take the action step to do it. In fact, you should begin every new conversation with a compliment. It is a wonderful way to start when you may be at a loss to break the ice. Everyone likes to hear a compliment when it is sincere.

Be Polite

Be polite to everyone you meet, and you'll find they respond with courtesy to you. I am respectful in all my relationships, to service providers as well as potential clients. I have gotten to know the managers at several New York restaurants, for example. Now whenever I call for a reservation, it is easier to get one. I nurture these relationships and stay "on their radar" through personal notes and gifts. Besides having a club to take clients and friends, it's nice to have several restaurants where I am always welcome. Try this. Your clients will be impressed, too!

Be polite to yourself as well. Thank yourself for your networking success—whether for attending an event and meeting some contacts you want to follow up with, landing a new job or a new piece of business as a result of a contact you developed into a trusted advisor or advocate. You deserve it! Watch, realize, and appreciate all the opportunities that have developed due to your new and improved networking awareness and good manners.

100/ Telephone Etiquette

In today's business world few things are as important as communicating your message in a professional manner. The telephone is one important tool used to find, grow, and keep business relationships. The rules of etiquette apply to telephone calls as well. Respect for your contacts' time and courteous listening skills are key. If you are uncomfortable on the telephone, write yourself a simple script and practice until it comes naturally. It is like having your "notes at the podium"—only they can't see them! To keep your calls from going too long, have a plan of action laid out for what you want to accomplish with each telephone call.

Here are some other quick telephone tips:

- ☉ Return all phone calls within 48 hours.
- ☉ When making a call, ask if it is a good time to talk. If not, schedule a more convenient time.
- ☉ State the purpose of your call and indicate you would like a few minutes of their time. Do not take any longer.
- ☉ When leaving a message, state your name, purpose, and action needed, clearly and succinctly. And most importantly, when leaving your phone number, speak slowly.
- ☉ When calling a contact referral, state your name and who referred you. For example, "Hello (name), my name is Andrea Nierenberg. (So and so) suggested I give you a call about . . ."
- ☉ Avoid multi-tasking while on the phone. People can hear you typing on your computer or shuffling papers. This shows you are not focused on them. Remember, "To do two things at once is to do neither."

101/ Meal Manners

Doing business at a lunch or dinner requires a set of etiquette rules. Here are a few important ones for meals with just you and your contact:

- ☉ When ordering, allow your guests to go first and select your entrée accordingly.
- ☉ The host directs the server first to the guests and then the host orders last.
- ☉ Leave your cell phone and Blackberry in your brief case, turned off. If you must accept an essential call, alert your host or guests when you sit down. When the call comes in, excuse yourself, and keep the conversation brief.
- ☉ The host should offer the option of dessert, even if you don't want it yourself.
- ☉ Keep the dinner napkin in your lap until you rise to leave the restaurant. If you leave the table, put the napkin in your chair until you return.
- ☉ Not sure which water glass or salad plate to use? Remem-

ber liquids on the right, solids on the left. If your neighbor forgets and takes yours, just ignore it.

⊙ If you are not sure which utensil to use first, working from the outside in is the safest bet.

⊙ When you are finished, place your knife and fork in a parallel position across the center of your plate. This signals for the waiter to clear your place. However, even if you are still hungry, stop eating when everyone else is finished. If you are a fast eater, slow your pace to match others.

⊙ Refrain from talking about business until after the appetizer course is removed. This allows time for getting acquainted. The servers will also be out of the way. You can finish your discussion over coffee.

⊙ It is perfectly acceptable to take notes at a business dinner or networking event, just ask first out of courtesy. Then use a small note pad, not an SUV-sized day planner.

⊙ Remember, always carry a mini etiquette survival kit with you: a note pad, pens, business cards, Kleenex, hand sanitizer, comb, and breath mints.

Meeting contacts at a larger business function involves a few more general etiquette rules: First introduce yourself to the person seated to your right and left. Then introduce yourself to the rest of the table. As others join your table, introduce yourself and others to one another. Also, wait for those at the head table to begin eating. Or, if at a private meal, wait for the host or hostess to begin. If you are the host or hostess, you must begin first.

102/ Other Etiquette Don'ts to Remember

⊙ Getting too personal
⊙ Complaining
⊙ Finishing other's sentences
⊙ Interrupting the other person
⊙ Using profanity or inappropriate jokes
⊙ Dressing inappropriately
⊙ Getting a mirror out at the table
⊙ Starting to discuss business too soon.

chapter 7

Leading the Way

Networking is a leadership skill; and to be a really successful leader, you need to continually hone these skills. Stand up and be a leader by accepting a position on the board of your professional or community organization. Raise your hand and volunteer to work on important projects and organize events, mentor new members or employees, teach a subject you know well at an organizational workshop or seminar. Arrange public speaking engagements for yourself to present your knowledge of a particular subject and show that you are a leader in your field. You can also try writing and publishing articles in professional or organizational publications to show you are a leader. Create your own Web site as a marketing tool and as a way to share your knowledge and expertise with others.

103/ Ways To Look like a Leader

What does a leader look like? You—especially if you have these leadership qualities:

1. **Great ATTITUDE**. Show you are interested in people and eager to learn more about them. Increase your attractiveness to others by actively listening and showing a sincere interest in what they have to say.
2. **Strong BELIEF.** You must have a firm knowledge of and belief in what you are promoting. Believe in yourself and your product or service.
3. **Passion.** Do what you love and love what you do. Once others can see that, things start to happen.You put the ball into motion.
4. **Ability to reach out and touch someone.** This is where your networking skills really come into play: You've learned

how to listen so you know how to help your contact and
you don't hesitate to do it.

5. **Ability to ask open-ended questions and listen to the
answers**. When you ask a question like: "How did you get
started in your business/profession?" You listen when they
tell their story. They have to know that you are truly interested.

6. **Ability to be unique.** What makes you different? This is
not only a key to successful networking, it will also be a
key to your business success. Be able to articulate first to
yourself and then to others about why someone may want
to utilize your services rather than your competitor.

7. **Ability to always have a gift.** Give more than you expect
to receive. Remember the Law of Reciprocity: No matter
how small the gift, they won't forget it. I'm firmly convinced
that those who give, receive other gifts in return from others in great abundance.

8. **Organizational skills.** Be a true Boy Scout or Girl Scout.
Always be ready for every occasion and be organized in
your workplace. Always carry a pen and business cards for
exchange or to write yourself notes for follow-up contacts.

9. **Ability to say "thank you" sincerely.** How many times
have you heard "Let's get together" or "I'll call you" and the
contact ends there? Take the initiative! Send a note or give
a call. Always make it from the heart.

10. **Ability to be real.** Most people have their own internal lie
detectors and can spot a phony a mile away. Don't activate
one, get out of your head and get into your heart!

104/ Ways to Act like a Leader Wherever You Are

How do you act like a leader? Follow these guidelines:

⊙ **Know that your reputation is valuable** and that it often
reaches people before you do. Be sincere, honest, prepared,
professional, thorough, efficient—and ***deliver***.

⊙ **Do what you say you're going to do.** Getting noticed
takes hard work, but it's a very small part of the total picture . . . you must also follow through!

⊙ **Return ALL phone calls.**

⊙ **Treat everyone with respect and courtesy.** A person's

position in life should have absolutely nothing to do with how you interact with them Remember what goes around comes around.

- ⊙ **Be visible.** Go to professional seminars, luncheons, receptions, dinners, any kind of gathering of folks.
- ⊙ **When you meet people, be mindful.** Look them in the eye, smile, be personable and have a firm handshake.
- ⊙ **Develop a knack for remembering names.** You'll be surprised at how positively people react when you remember their name after only a brief introduction. It also helps to take good notes about things you learned from a previous encounter, so you can remember them next time you meet a contact. Information on family, important dates, recent key events or projects can all be included in a computer file to jog your memory, and show you're interested.
- ⊙ **Be an active listener.** This has been discussed a number of times in this book, so you know how important it is.
- ⊙ **Create a "small talk" notebook**, which contains anecdotes and/or questions you've jotted down about life or current events that are guaranteed to stimulate conversation.
- ⊙ **Be sensitive to the body language** of those with whom you come in contact. And be aware of how you come across to others.
- ⊙ **Send a follow-up note** to people you've met with whom you'd like to keep in touch.
- ⊙ **Get to know the support staff** of the person or company with which you want to do business.
- ⊙ **Know your profession.** Stay abreast of all the latest trends and developments in your field and your geographic area. Read everything you can get your hands on and know who is doing what, where, when, and how.
- ⊙ **Pass articles along with a note** if you come across one that may be of interest to a co-worker or colleague.
- ⊙ **Keep a supply of greeting cards** for all occasions.
- ⊙ **Write, write, write.** Send letters to people you want to do business with. Say, "Hello," "Congratulations," "I like your work/your style/your recent remarks/your . . ."
- ⊙ **Go through your business contact list or database periodically** and send a hello note to those people you want to remember you.

- ⊙ **Let people know that you are available** to speak or participate in panel discussions, seminars, clubs, religious organizations, civic groups, charitable organizations, service groups, and community centers.
- ⊙ **Selectively donate your services** to non-profit organizations that may be in need of your expertise. Give of your time and expertise generously. Be known as the "go to" person for your particular specialty. Remember to be a resource to others.
- ⊙ **Remember what Mom used to tell you** . . . say "thank you." It's amazing how few people invest the time to express gratitude for a favor or a job well done. Remember that people *don't have to do anything* for you. Develop a "thank you" style that is flexible and works for you, then make this professional courtesy a habit. It will make you stand up in a world where so few people take the time or the trouble to do this.

One day as I walked past the North Fork Bank in New York City, I spotted two business books through their huge picture window—neither one of them was my book! I walked right in and handed a copy of *Million Dollar Networking* to the vice president's assistant, saying cheerfully, "I'd like to give Mr. Gambino a copy of my book."

She looked at me, then asked me to wait as she went in and gave it to him. When I was invited into his office, I said: "I have guts. I just thought I would bring you another business book!"

He said, "I like people with guts!"

Since then, Carl Gambino has kept my book right in the picture window so that it is seen every day by many; and I have done work with his bank and through him have made many other great connections.

Be a leader. Take the initiative!!

105/ Be a Leader at Business Functions

How do you recognize leaders at a business function? Here are the qualities that them stand out:

- ⊙ Ability to make others feel comfortable
- ⊙ Appear confident and at ease
- ⊙ Ability to laugh at themselves—not at others

- Show interest in others: maintain eye contact, self-disclose, ask questions, and actively listen
- Extend themselves to others—lean into a greeting with a firm handshake and a smile
- Convey a sense of enthusiasm and energy
- Are well rounded, well informed, well intentioned, and well mannered
- Know vignettes or stories of actual events that are interesting, humorous, and appropriate
- Convey respect and genuinely like people.

Leadership Qualities for the Office
- Keep it professional all the time
- Know the protocol of the firm
- Listen more than you speak
- Don't criticize others
- Help others get what they want
- Create win/win solutions
- Be assertive—not aggressive
- Be willing to go the extra mile
- Be appreciative of the help you get
- Work with dedication and loyalty
- Constantly improve your knowledge
- Be the best at what you do
- Learn to get along with everyone
- Be diplomatic.

106/ Show Networking Leadership in Your Own Office

When the economy is hot, people leave companies without hesitation for more money and/or more prestige. Yet studies still show us that money is not the only motivator that keeps people loyal and productive at their current company.

As long as you are paying your people a decent wage and up to the market's standards, there are a few very simple grassroot steps that managers can take to keep their best employees on the payroll and happy to be there. . . and networking skills will help you.

Here are some great "networking" ways to motivate your team—without monetary reward:

1. A word of thanks—yes, a sincere thank you from the right

person (you) at the right time can mean a lot to a member of your team. Part of the power of this thanks comes because you took the time to note some achievement they've made. Do it several ways—tell the person, write them a card, and here's a special tip—send it to their home so that their spouse or family can share in the gratitude. This goes a long way, and it is only human nature that people will respect it.

2. Give praise. As the saying goes—praise pays. Tell your staff what they did right and be specific. Know their communication style and deliver the message in the way they understand it. Some people like public praise, others find it is embarrassing. Honor your employee by knowing which one they will accept. Remember to give credit where it's due and consider starting a recognition award in your company. Mary Kay Ash, the founder of Mary Kay Cosmetics, said there are two things people want more than sex and money—praise and recognition!

3. Become a great listener. Make regular eye contact with an employee when he or she is confiding in you. Ask open-ended questions for clarification. Show concern. Restate or paraphrase back what they've said. Pay close attention and do not let your mind wander. Don't interrupt!

4. Follow through. If you promise something, deliver. This is how trust and loyalty are built.

107/ "Who Packed Your Parachute?"

Many people only speak to or connect with people they think are important. I'm here to tell you that in order to be a successful networker and leader, everyone must be important.

Consider the story of Charles Plumb who was a U.S. Navy jet pilot during the Vietnam War. He spent time in a prison because after 75 combat missions, his plane was hit and he was ejected and parachuted to safety—into the arms of the Viet Cong, however.

Some years after he was released, he and his wife were out to dinner one night when a man approached him and said, "You're Plumb, and you flew jet fighters in Vietnam from the aircraft carrier Kitty Hawk. You were shot down!" Plumb looked at him in astonishment and asked how he knew.

"I packed your parachute," the man replied. "I guess it worked!"

Plumb gasped both in surprise and gratitude.

That night he could not sleep. He wondered what that parachute-packer had looked like in a Navy uniform. "Did I ever say 'good morning' to him? I hope I didn't ignore him because I was a fighter pilot and he was 'just' a sailor." He thought about how hard this fellow and others like him had worked, making sure that the chute would open. They'd actually held the fate of a flyer they didn't know in their hands. As a public speaker, Plumb began asking his audiences, "Who packs your parachute?"

We all have people who help us get through the day in every way and very often in small, yet major ways. Take the time to keep people in your sights, no matter how busy you are facing the challenges of life. Say hello, please, and thank you, congratulate someone on something that has happened to them, give a compliment, or just do something nice for no reason. This tip packs volumes— just do it!

108/ Organizing and Keeping Track of Your Network

Leaders keep records about all their contacts, so they can respond to them as individuals. There are some great new software packages that you can customize to your needs, or keep index cards if that suits you better. You must develop your own system to keep in touch with everyone in your network on a regular basis. As your list grows, divide it into categories and have a contact plan for each one. Quality versus quantity. Make sure you "touch" those closest to you often.

Regularly review your contact list and "clean out" those contacts who, for whatever reason, are no longer in your life. Last summer I had what I thought was a major setback. While I was overseas and my newsletter was being sent out back home, somehow the new server we used was a bit careless and someone hit the wrong button. This resulted in me becoming a "spam queen" in minutes. I was mortified and did not know what to do except send a massive apology. Afterward, I decided to really comb through the list. I had over 5,000 names on it. Some were people to whom others had forwarded the newsletter so the list had continued growing.

I decided to rebuild organically with people who first wanted to be in touch and get my newsletter and those who asked to be on it. It has now grown to 2,000 names and keeps growing, yet I do know every person who is on there now.

Make and record notes about each meeting with someone and refer to your notes when communicating. This is easily done on your contact management system and can be linked to your handheld device for easy access when you're on the road. I download this continually from my Outlook to my Blackberry. I have all my information at hand and updated all the time.

Develop your system for filing business cards depending on how you plan to use them in the future. Enter them into your database with special notes for follow up. Take action now. I am a true stickler on this one.

Refer back to chapter 4 for a handy list of all the information I gather for each of my contacts. Into my computer database, I first enter basic contact information: name, title, company, address, phone, fax, cell phone, and e-mail. In a separate field, I then enter the contacts preferred method of communication: "E" for e-mail, "V" for voice mail or "P" for phone.

Other information I know about them goes in the "details" section. In the "activities" section I enter information such as work-related information, personal interests, what food they like, what books they like, a favorite restaurant, sports activities, and family information including names of spouse and children.

I add categories as necessary that are helpful for sorting such as:

- Category, i.e., client, prospect, supplier, professional, or personal
- "Hot" contact: need to follow up more frequently
- Source of contact: referral, organization, event, meeting, etc.
- Ideas and referrals they have given me: including thank-you chain contacts
- Gift history: gifts and premiums sent, date, occasion
- Holiday cards sent
- Designation as A, B, or C (my method of prioritizing contacts)

109/ Be a Leader for Your Customers: The 7/11 Rule

In the first 7 seconds of contact, a customer forms 11 impressions about you and your organization. Is it "fair?" No, and are they sometimes wrong. Yes, it's a common human trait.

Here's what they'll rate you on:

1. Opening impression: friendly and open
2. Attractive
3. Credible
4. Knowledgeable
5. Responsive
6. Friendly
7. Empathetic
8. Courteous
9. Confident
10. Professional
11. Helpful

. . . and they make one of three decisions:

1. They dislike you
2. They are indifferent
3. They love you.

Now review the leadership qualities we've been discussing, and you'll know how to look like the kind of leader customers trust.

110/ Think Client Retention

Client value is the total benefit (tangible and intangible) that you, your business partners, and your coalition provide to a client throughout the life of the relationship. There's no better way to gain perspective on each and every client relationship, or to predict the impact of every management decision on long-term revenue goals.

⊙ Identify and document your ideal customer. Get very specific. What are their job functions, key frustrations, buying behavior, lifestyle, age, willingness to advise you on new offerings, and typical spending habits with your firm? Do they value expertise and are they willing to pay a premium for good service, or are they transactional buyers who only care about price (a la Wal-Mart)? Write down the percentage of firms in your portfolio that fit each description.

- Keep a journal for one week detailing how much time you're spending with your ideal customer. The next week, track how much time you are spending with your "less than ideal" customer. The third week, list three ways you can stream-line the way you work with your "less than ideal" customer, beginning one month from the day you make the list. This may include everything from referring them to another firm to delegating them to a more junior associate, to asking them to pay you in a more efficient way (paypal.com), etc.

- Guesstimate how much your ideal customer will buy from you during the entire buyer/seller relationship. For ex-ample, if you are a consultant, and a typical client stays with you for two years, paying you $10,000 a month, then the current lifetime direct transaction value of a client is $10,000 x 24 months = $240,000.

- Guesstimate how much business each client will refer to you over the next two years. Let's say the typical client sends you one new client every two years at $10,000 a month. That's $240,000 in referral value.

- If you have an advisory team of customers helping you design or launch new products or services, estimate the value of one successful sale for that new offering based on your customers' input.

- Provide your ideal clients with one free service, trial offer, or referral—just to show them how much you value the relationship. No expectations, period. Make this year your season for giving unconditionally.

- Create and regularly administer a low-cost survey to find out how your ideal clients define, receive, and measure value.

- Create a "Master Mind" group of professionals within your organization dedicated exclusively to defining, attracting, and creating lifelong clients and learning from each other.

- Create a referral network of companies, clients, and indi-viduals. Share this with your clients and update it often.

Client retention and development are critical to all we are dis-cussing in this book. You work hard to build, develop, and keep your relationships. This is what a true leader thinks about. One of my favorite quotes is: A leader is a good manager, yet a manager is not always a good leader. Decide which you are.

111/ The POWER of Preparation

The trick is to be prepared, have your plan of action, stay calm, and ask for what you want. Here's how to do it with authority and P.O.W.E.R:

P "Prepare, prepare, prepare," said Winston Churchill. Essentially when you make a call, you are making a pitch or a presentation. Prepare in advance what you want to say.

O Develop an outline from beginning to end. Know what you want to say from beginning to end.

W Walk in the customer's shoes. When you speak with your client, hear them out and listen. You will learn something during the process.

E Enter the stage, strongly and confidently. Shakespeare said that we're all actors on this stage called life. If your client is like a lion and your approach is like a lamb, you might be devoured!

R Rapport will build bridges. You've heard the expression, love your friends and love your enemies more. Build the relationship.

In any case, the P.O.W.E.R. you have is often in your hands. Take action!

This story actually happened to me in 1976 when I was just out of training. Back then, a $5,000 order was considered large and average production was less than $50,000 per year.

We had spent five weeks in New York for training. A few months later I scheduled a seminar to discuss utility stocks with a group of ten potential investors. One of the ladies I'd been talking to didn't show up. So the next day I called her and she said she was sorry that she could not attend, something had come up at the last minute. I then went over the points of the utility we'd featured. She said that she wanted to meet me before she would do any business. We agreed I would come by her home on the way to work the next morning.

At 9:00 a.m. I was knocking at her door—the only doublewide trailer in the park. She invited me in and after

*a few minutes we were discussing utilities. "What's this I
hear about municipal bonds being tax free and how does
someone buy them?" she asked me. I showed her the unit
trust format, explaining that they pay monthly and cost about
a thousand dollars apiece. She said she liked that, and she
wanted a hundred of them.*

*I was taken aback because I couldn't conceive of an or-
der that large. "You know that will be $100,000," I warned her.
She immediately responded, "I know what $100,000 is."*

*I said, "Of course you do." Then I told her my manager
would require a deposit. She said, "Of course, he will." She
walked to her extra bedroom where she had a safe and
brought me $40,000 in cash.*

"Will that be enough?"

*Yes, I responded. She asked for a receipt. "I'll have to
write it on the back of my business card. Is that OK?" Sure,
she said. "Could I borrow a paper bag to put the money in?
My briefcase wont' hold it." She gave me the bag. It took me
two hours to count it since it was all in twenties.*

*It was now 11:30 a.m. and I headed to the office. The
manager required me to be there at 8:00, so I thought I would
play a joke on him. I wandered into the office. He immediately called me into his office and asked where I'd been. I
said that my career was starting off too slowly, so on the
way to work, I'd robbed a bank. I dumped the money on his
desk. He immediately went into shock. It took fifteen minutes to convince him of my comedian talents. He finally
calmed down and was happy because I had now become
the office leader for the month.*

*This is a true story, and from that point forward I al-
ways felt comfortable asking for the large orders and my
career has been very successful since.*

—Stephen E. Woeber, Morgan Stanley,
The Woeber Snyder Group

112/ Executive Networking: The Next Step Up

1. **Go where other senior execs go.** Attend professional and
   industry meetings specifically targeted for your executive status. While general networking meetings at your

local industry might be excellent for your staff; your time is better used mixing with other senior people from different companies to help open doors for your front-line people.

2. **Pursue high net worth hobbies.** Many senior executives meet at the golf club, country club, tennis court, or fundraising art gallery opening. Figure out your interests and then get involved.

3. **Volunteer to speak.** Share your industry knowledge, but research the profiles of attendees before offering yourself as a speaker to make sure these are the type of new contacts you need to impress.

4. **Do some internal research.** For instance, touch base with your sales and marketing staff to find out what history your company has with some of the business leaders you'll be meeting. This way, if there is something good to bring up, you can use it during your conversation.

5. **Prepare your self-marketing message.** Your company is key. However, your personal message can really be a door opener. Think about your personal experiences and background that will be of interest to your peers. It might be related to labor relations or how you coped with new government regulations. Show how you creatively handled problems that you know others are facing and become a resource.

As a senior executive you are in a unique place to foster, build, and cultivate new relationships. Just remember that networking is a process that, with respect and patience, can create business connections to last a lifetime.

Here is how I connected with one client, which then led to another. I went to an open house reception hosted by a law firm that had recently moved its offices. While there I met an attorney whom I had not seen in five years. I told her that I had gone into business on my own, serving as the interim CEO for nonprofits undergoing executive transition.

The next evening, she had dinner with a friend of hers, who is another lawyer I know whom I had not seen in ten years. She told that lawyer that she had run into me and let her know what I was doing. A few days later, that second lawyer had lunch with the CEO of a nonprofit she represents. The CEO advised her that she had given notice, and that the nonprofit needed an interim CEO. The lawyer recommended me to the Board's president, and I was hired a week later.

I served for nine months as the interim CEO at this organization. During that time, I had occasion to be introduced to someone at a meeting with the City Health Commissioner. After I left the organization, this person referred me to an office colleague of his who happened to be a board member of another nonprofit, which became my next client.

—John Corwin, Corwin Consulting, LLC

113/ Leadership Techniques at Trade Shows or Conferences

Realize that all eyes are on you. Trade shows are like big supermarkets; people are going down the aisles looking for the products that are most appealing. Assuming that all the booths have dynamite fixtures and support materials, then the only thing separating them are the people. Customers start making an impression of you 30 feet from your booth as they're approaching.

Here are some ways to get their attention:

1. **Smile**. It disarms almost everybody. Make your smile sincere and warm, and be genuinely happy to see the visitors as they approach your booth. It's a great opener to see a pleasant and enthusiastic face.

2. **Stand tall**. We project more confidence and demonstrate that we are interested in meeting the people when we stand, rather than sit. We've all seen salespeople who are lounging in their chairs and look like the last thing they want to do is get up and greet someone.

3. **Keep your mouth free of food, drink, and chewing gum**. Eat only at your breaks; and when you do, make the snack or meal healthy and light. The last thing you want is to appear lethargic at the booth. Also, stock up on bottled water, breath mints, and power bars. Be careful of eating fatty foods that slow you down, and also avoid getting "wired" by drinking too much coffee.

4. **Make sure you look marvelous**. While a trade show is

one place that demands dressing professionally, keep comfort in mind as well. Tight-fitting clothing will definitely impact your comfort while selling. And if you're wearing something that has pockets, avoid putting your hands in them, it makes you look unapproachable.

5. **Your feet will have an impact on the rest of your body**. Wear comfortable shoes because you'll be on your feet all day. This is also not the time to break in a pair of new shoes. There are too many stories of those who left the show at night practically crippled with blisters and sores from not wearing the right shoes.

6. **Wear your badge on your right side**. The reason is that our eyes naturally flow in the same direction as the person's hand we're shaking, which makes it easier for people to see your name tag. Also be careful to shake in a firm and professional manner. If your palms sweat, dry them off periodically so clients don't get a clammy grip.

7. **Speak with your guests and not to your fellow "exhibitors."** Make it easy for people to come up to the booth. By nature, people don't like to approach strangers in a group. When you do engage in a conversation with a prospect, listen more than you speak. Remember, in person you have the advantage of watching his or her body language. Determine if what the other person says matches how he or she feels about working with you.

8. **Perception is reality**. Your booth area is a reflection of you and your company. Keep it clean, neat, and orderly. Be careful not to give away too much literature to everyone who walks by. Instead, be particular, and only give people what they specifically have an interest in. Remember that you can always send information to them after the show.

Studies tell us that most of your collateral material ends up in the wastebasket because the attendees want to carry home as little as possible. They know you'll follow up and send it to them anyway. Research has shown that you'll have a 50 percent better chance of having it read if you mail it to them after the show. This also gives you a reason to follow up with a telephone call to find out if they have received the information.

114/ Techniques to Separate You From the Tradeshow Competition

- ⊙ **The name game**. We all would like to be able to remember names better, especially at a trade show where you're meeting many new people. Practice some of the techniques described in previous chapters, like keeping eye contact so you remember their face, repeating their name when you respond to an introduction, and associating something else with their name.

- ⊙ **Postcards from the show**. Imagine being one of your prime prospects or clients. You come home from a show and are inundated with salespeople mailing you all the typical follow-up catalogs and brochures. How can you stand out? Send clients a postcard from the city you've just been visiting. Now think of this: Mr. Client returns back to his office several days later, and as he glances through the mail, he sees a postcard from Chicago, from which he has just returned. He turns it over and it says, "Dear Mr. Client: It was great seeing you at the show. Thanks for your time. As suggested, I'll follow up in the next week. All my best." Now, do you think you'll be remembered among all the other people who saw him at the show? Yes. I do this daily at the shows. I send out about 25 postcards at the end of each day so that I'm sure the postcards will get to them in a timely fashion.

- ⊙ **Give yourself a break**. Trade shows can be stressful and can take their toll on us if we're not careful. Here are a few tips to practice everyday:

1. Do some deep breathing exercises to clear your head.
2. Eat well-balanced meals and avoid excessive amounts of sugar, caffeine, fat, salt, and additives.
3. Get enough rest. Have the discipline to decline a few late night parties or outings. Remember, if planned correctly, you'll know what meetings are critical and which are less important.
4. Get some exercise. Most hotels have an exercise room. This might even be another alternative selling

opportunity. I've met contacts next to me on the Stairmaster.

⊙ **There's no place like home**. Bring part of your home environment with you like pictures of loved ones, your own pillow, fresh flowers in your room, a CD player with some of your favorite music.

The idea of maximizing your trade show efforts is to have a plan, be organized, pace yourself, and work smart so that you bring home some bottom-line benefits.

115/ Tips for Success as You Battle Through the Trade Shows

⊙ Smile. It's the universal greeting.
⊙ Have fun working. Be patient and inject humor when possible.
⊙ Keep it simple. Find ways to simplify the selling process.
⊙ Show character. It takes forever to build relationships, and they can be ruined by one improper action or word.
⊙ Be kind and nice to everyone you meet at the show.
⊙ Make your company proud by demonstrating the best customer service.
⊙ Do what you promised to do after the show.
⊙ Be economical. Watch your expenses on the road; most things cost more than at home.
⊙ Be patient. Everyone may not respond positively to you the first time; give people time.
⊙ Work to improve selling efforts at the booth. You may need to revise your plan as the show progresses.
⊙ Be original and unique. Find out what parts of your personality people respond to positively.

Before we finish, here are some questions that can help you better plan the next trade show:

1. What pre-show planning would you do now that you have not thought of before?

2. How do define the purpose of attending a trade show?

_____

3. What can you plan at an exhibition that will directly improve sales?

_____

4. How can you upstage the competition?

_____

5. What has your company done in the past that has succeeded or failed at trade shows?

_____

Booth camp is now over. When you follow these techniques, you'll find yourself in better shape to win over customers.

116/ Secret Qualities Of Great Business Communications

The mysterious qualities that make one person charismatic and likeable and another less so have been contemplated by philosophers and business people throughout the years. Listed below are seven qualities that the finest communicators *always* possess. They . . .

- ⊙ Are confident and unafraid to ask for what they want
- ⊙ Appreciate those that help them
- ⊙ Consistently nurture relationships
- ⊙ Are tenacious in going around obstacles
- ⊙ Are excellent listeners
- ⊙ Rebound quickly and completely from rejection
- ⊙ Are friendly and approachable.

Don't forget these tips for managing your e-mail correspondence.

- ⊙ Set aside a specific time (or times) in the day to read and answer emails.
- ⊙ Use the "in-box" method:
  1. Answer immediately all that you can.
  2. Forward those that can be handled by others.
  3. Save newsletters and other reading material for later in the day.
  4. Delete the rest.

  If I have to read a message later, I save it as "new."

117/ Motivation for Change

You CAN change your life! For each area of your life (family, career, health etc.) ask yourself:

- ⊙ What do I want to start doing?
- ⊙ What do I want to stop doing?
- ⊙ What do I want to keep doing?
- ⊙ Start making *active choices*. So much of what we do, we do without thinking. Let's say you have set a goal for yourself of more money in the bank. You are out shopping and suddenly you find yourself preparing to buy something you don't need. Ask yourself: Do I want more money in the bank or do I want this product? Make an active choice based on your own goals.
- ⊙ Learn to say "no." We have been taught to say yes. Saying yes means our lives are often too busy with things we don't want, so there is no room for the things we do want. Saying no means focusing on the things you do want. This one takes practice. Say "no" in a positive way.
- ⊙ Find role models. When you really like what someone stands for, what their legacy is, pay attention and find ways to model your life on theirs.
- ⊙ Focus on what you want, *not on what you don't want*. There is a saying that *what you focus on grows*. So if you are busy focusing on what you don't want to have, then you are focusing on the negative. Focus instead on the positive and notice how things change, including the way you feel about it.
- ⊙ Take it *one step at a time*. Making changes in our lives is like learning to walk as a baby: You've got to focus on the positive, follow your instincts, and take it one step at a time!
- ⊙ Leverage it up. Start where you are and work your way up. Take an honest and realistic assessment of where you are now and start from there. Leverage what you have now into something more. Take your current skills and expand them. Find ways to make them grow into what you want them to be.
- ⊙ Be GREATFUL and be grateful. Be full of your own *greatness* and be grateful that you have it. Being full of your

own greatness doesn't mean having a huge ego! It does mean recognizing and accepting that you are great . . . at one thing or several things.

- ⊙ Be prepared. We are so often running around trying to catch up that being prepared seems a dream. Being prepared is the single most important thing you can do to increase your personal effectiveness. Making time to be prepared means slowing down to the pace of life. It will allow you to enjoy the moment, be connected, and be in tune with what is happening around you. It will also demonstrate your leadership.
- ⊙ Laugh—find humor everywhere. Laughter is an incredible thing. Find ways to laugh everyday. Find humor in a situation where you never saw humor before.

118/ Excuses or Blockers to Leadership

Now that you've read about leadership, do you still find yourself excusing yourself from getting on with success by saying:

- ⊙ Not enough money
- ⊙ Too much effort to do . . . consistently
- ⊙ I have a language or cultural barrier
- ⊙ I already do TOO much to do all these things.

I hear these a lot and I realize that we all make many choices in life. Some of us have less or more on our plates than others. Which is why I say: "Take the best and leave the rest." Do just one new thing or add one new tip into your life and make it work for you. It can even be an "aha" in that you say: "I am already doing this. I just didn't know it was networking or relationship marketing." Make it work for you in your life.

You have the chance to learn something valuable today. Whether the day is frenzied or peaceful, stressful or relaxing, there is much you can learn from the living of it. Some people let life's lessons slip by unnoticed. Others take them to heart, eagerly and often. Life offers its lessons to all. And life richly rewards those who accept and appreciate them. You could complain that something doesn't work, or you could learn to make it work. You can allow the setbacks to discourage you, or you can let the setbacks teach you how to get ahead.

From every experience there is a lesson. From every person, from every situation, from every success, and especially from every disappointment, there is something to be learned. Learn all you can from those lessons.

Master life's lessons, and you'll surely master life.
—Ralph Marston